What is Social Network Analysis?

'What is?' Research Methods series

Edited by Graham Crow, University of Southampton
ISSN: 2048–6812

The 'What is?' series provides authoritative introductions to a range of research methods which are at the forefront of developments in the social sciences. Each volume sets out the key elements of the particular method and features examples of its application, drawing on a consistent structure across the whole series. Written in an accessible style by leading experts in the field, this series is an innovative pedagogical and research resource.

What is Online Research?
Tristram Hooley, John Marriott and Jane Wellens

What is Social Network Analysis?
John Scott

What is Qualitative Research?
Martyn Hammersley

What is Discourse Analysis?
Stephanie Taylor

What are Qualitative Research Ethics?
Rose Wiles

What are Community Studies?
Graham Crow

Forthcoming books:

What is Qualitative Interviewing?
Rosalind Edwards and Janet Holland

What is Narrative Research?
Molly Andrews, Mark Davis, Cigdem Esin, Lar-Christer Hyden, Margareta Hyden, Corinne Squire and Barbara Harrison

What is Inclusive Research?
Melanie Nind

What is
social network
analysis?

John Scott

BLOOMSBURY ACADEMIC

First published in 2012 by

Bloomsbury Academic

an imprint of Bloomsbury Publishing Plc
50 Bedford Square, London WC1B 3DP, UK
and
175 Fifth Avenue, New York, NY 10010, USA

CIP records for this book are available from the British Library and the
Library of Congress

ISBN 978-1-78093-848-6 (hardback)
ISBN 978-1-84966-817-0 (paperback)
ISBN 978-1-84966-819-4 (ebook)

This book is produced using paper that is made from wood grown in managed,
sustainable forests. It is natural, renewable and recyclable. The logging and
manufacturing processes conform to the environmental regulations of
the country of origin.

Printed and bound in Great Britain by MPG Books Group, Bodmin, Cornwall.

Cover design: Burge Agency

www.bloomsburyacademic.com

Contents

Contents

List of Figures

Series foreword

The idea behind this series is a simple one: to provide concise and accessible overviews of a range of frequently-used research methods and of current issues in research methodology. Books in the series have been written by experts in their fields with a brief to write about their subject for a broad audience who are assumed to be interested but not necessarily to have any prior knowledge. The series is a natural development of presentations made in the 'What is?' strand at Economic and Social Research Council Research Methods Festivals which have proved popular both at the Festivals themselves and subsequently as a resource on the website of the ESRC National Centre for Research Methods.

Methodological innovation is the order of the day, and the 'What is?' format allows researchers who are new to a field to gain an insight into its key features, while also providing a useful update on recent developments for people who have had some prior acquaintance with it. All readers should find it helpful to be taken through the discussion of key terms, the history of how the method or methodological issue has developed, and the assessment of the strengths and possible weaknesses of the approach through analysis of illustrative examples.

The examples considered here relating to the process of innovation, the nature of relations within a community, and the operation of power are only a fraction of the social phenomena whose character can be illuminated by social network analysis, but they are enough to establish that networks deserve to be taken seriously by anyone seeking to understand how the social world works. The book also demonstrates how the growing methodological rigour of social network analysis has not been at the expense of comprehensibility; the underlying ideas that people are connected through networks but that these networks may be hidden to outsiders remain powerful and persuasive ones.

The books cannot provide information about their subject matter down to a fine level of detail, but they will equip readers with a powerful sense of reasons why it deserves to be taken seriously and, it is hoped, with the enthusiasm to put that knowledge into practice.

Graham Crow
Series editor

1 Introduction

Social network analysis conceptualises individuals or groups as 'points' and their relations to each other as 'lines'. It is concerned with the patterns formed by the points and lines and involves exploring these patterns, mathematically or visually, in order to assess their effects on the individuals and organisations that are the members of the 'networks' formed by the intersecting lines that connect them. It therefore takes the metaphorical idea of interaction as forming a network of connections and gives this idea a more formal representation in order to model structures of social relations. Treating a social structure as a network is the cornerstone of social network analysis.

Social network analysis has changed a lot in the last forty years and the network analyst of today works very differently from the one of the early 1970s. In this book I will trace these changes from the early origins of the approach in simple metaphorical ideas to the contemporary rigour and formalism that characterises it. My own involvement in network analysis over this period has meant that I have myself experienced the changes that have led to the highly technical and sophisticated measures that now face the newcomer. The book can usefully begin, therefore, with a contrast between how it was done before and how it is done now.

My personal interest in social network analysis began because I had an interest in economic power and a fascination with the work of those who claimed to have identified the key financial groups in contemporary economies and to have shown the webs of connection that tied them together through class-based links of schooling, club membership, and kinship. It seemed to me that this could best be studied through an investigation of interlocking directorships and through the use of systematic network methods. Small studies by Richard Whitley (1973) and by Phil Stanworth and Tony Giddens (1975) were beginning to appear at this time, and these authors had drawn diagrams of board connections among small numbers of companies and had reported the measured 'density' of their networks. These studies seemed to offer an advantage over the more popular diagrammatic representations produced by radical journalists in which the nature of the connections and the implications of the patterns were not considered. However, I felt that there had to be a way of extending these systematic methods to the larger selections of companies that I wanted to study.

The early 1970s were a time at which British sociology was beginning to make advances in the use of mathematical techniques to study individuals and their relationships. The British Sociological Association Quantitative Sociology Group had been formed as a focus for this work and I wrote a short piece for its newsletter in which I requested help in my search for useable techniques of social network analysis. This brought me into contact with leading figures in North America, Britain, and continental Europe: Barry Wellman, Joel Levine, Mike Schwartz, Frans Stokman, Rob Mokken, Clyde Mitchell, and Tony Coxon all made the 'first contact' between 1975 and 1976 that allowed me to boldly go across this new frontier of sociological methods. From these people I learned ideas, acquired programs, and received much needed intellectual support. I learned of possible measures and of computer programs that could, with some difficulty, help me in my task.

Before I could undertake any social network analysis, however, I had to collect some data. My data collection had begun some years previously when I began a project on ownership and control in the Scottish economy and the involvement of Scottish companies in the development of the oil and gas resources of the North Sea (published in Scott and Hughes 1976; 1980). Arriving at a list of companies to study was easy, and it was then fairly straightforward to compile lists of the names of their directors. Two sets of record cards were produced: (1) a set of company cards, one for each company, recording the names of all the directors in each company; (2) a set of director cards, one for each director, recording the names of all the companies on which the director sat. The second set of cards was difficult to produce, as it involved searching through all the company cards to identify any person who appeared on more than one company card. This involved a manual, error-prone process of spotting similar names and then searching a variety of sources in order to discover whether J. Smith, John Smith, H. John Smith, and Brigadier General H. J. Smith were all, in fact, the same person or needed to be treated separately. An additional problem was that company information had been reported in the directories used at various dates during the year and so John Smith may have become Sir John Smith, Lord Smith, or even Lord Tottenham, part of the way through the year. Not for some years was it possible to enter the company and director names into a computer and to sort them automatically into alphabetical order so as to bring similar names closer together in the list.

When a reasonably clean data set had been produced, some quantitative analysis could begin. This involved manually sorting the cards into piles on the floor in order to calculate frequencies: for example, the numbers of directors with 2, 3, 4, or more directorships in the companies studied, and the numbers of companies with boards of particular sizes or numbers of 'multiple directors'. This task, too, was soon helped by my investment in a pocket calculator. However, many network measures that are now standard could not be produced in this way and I had to resort to drawing network diagrams by hand—using long rolls of wallpaper—in order to map out the principal connections. These diagrams served an interpretative purpose for me as a researcher, allowing me to identify the well-connected and the less well-connected companies and to recognise areas of intense connection but they were impossible to use as means of rigorous data analysis or for presentation to others. I explored various simplified diagrams that gave 'artist's impressions' of the data in the hope that I could clarify the broad structure of the large network, but none of these proved satisfactory.

Once I had access to computer programs from the colleagues who had contacted me, things became a lot easier. For a study of British companies (Scott and Griff 1984) I transferred the data onto punched cards which could then be read into the university's mainframe Control Data Corporation (CDC) Cyber computer. The British project came to form a part of an international project headed by Frans Stokman, who headed the team that had produced a network program called GRAph Definition and Analysis Package (GRADAP), also stored on a larger CDC computer at Gröningen University. My punched cards were transferred to a large data tape, and this was posted to Gröningen for analysis there—no other computer was large enough to handle the program and its data. A few weeks later I would begin to receive the output in the form of reams of computer printout on concertinaed paper.

The output received was, however, a revelation. Most of the now-standard network concepts could be generated by GRADAP, and I could begin to report the basic structural features of my network—a mere three years or so after I had begun to compile the data. All the researchers in the ten participating countries worked in the same way and the Gröningen team produced equivalent output for each participant, so ensuring strict comparability in the analysis of our various data sets.

Some measures were not, however, included in GRADAP. For these I relied on a program written by Clyde Mitchell. Clyde provided me with a copy of the program—CONCOR—on punched cards and the university computer staff wrote a small program that could convert my GRADAP files into a form suitable for use with CONCOR. The computer demands for CONCOR were so great that it could run only because my university rented time on the Manchester super-computer: which was almost as powerful as one of today's mobile phones! Each time I used the program I consumed a half of the university's weekly budget, and each time I made a mistake in punching the cards—which was often—I had to rerun the program, sometimes a week later, when more budget was available. The physicists who regarded all computers as their sole property were none too pleased about this.

Since personal computers became more easily available from the late 1980s, the research process has changed dramatically. Pioneers of contemporary social network analysis have produced cheap software that can be run on any desktop. The initial steps still require a great deal of manual cleaning of the data, even when these have been harvested directly from an online data source. Standard computer software also allows easy conversion and transfer of data. Analyses that would have required an overnight run on the Manchester super-computer in 1984 can now be analysed on a laptop in less than a second. Some networking procedures are now routinely implemented on mobile phones on a daily basis by anyone who uses Facebook. Newcomers to social network analysis are able to start their work more quickly and more easily than ever before.

These changes are what make this book timely. I have tried to produce a simple primer that introduces and illustrates the basic ideas of social network analysis and that will allow users to quickly use the software themselves and to move on to more advanced introductions that will give a deeper understanding of the concepts and measures that are being used.

2 History of social network analysis

The roots of social network thinking are to be found in relational or structural approaches to social analysis that developed in classical sociology. While some approaches to sociology and anthropology used the ideas of culture and cultural formation to explain social patterns of feeling, thought, and behaviour, and others stressed the material environment and the physicality of the body as crucial determinants, a particularly important strand of social thought focused its attention on the actual patterns of interaction and interconnection through which individuals and social groups are related to each other. In some cases this involved a conception of the 'social organism', or social system, as a structure of institutions that constrain the subjectivity and actions of those who occupy positions within those institutions. For other theorists, however, greater attention was given to the immediate face-to-face encounters through which individuals relate to each other and that are constantly refigured through the actions of these individuals.

It was among the latter theorists that the metaphors of the social 'network' and its equivalents—such as the social 'web' or the social 'fabric'—first emerged. German social theorists such as Ferdinand Tönnies and Georg Simmel took up this idea in their 'formal sociology', seen as a sociology of the 'forms' of interaction that carry and contain the diverse subjectively meaningful contents that motivate the actions of individuals. The translation of this work and the publication of much of it in the *American Journal of Sociology* encouraged many US sociologists of the first decade of the twentieth century to pursue an 'interactionist' approach to social life. Charles Cooley, Albion Small and George Mead were, perhaps, the leading figures in this movement of thought. In Germany itself, the sociologies of Alfred Vierkandt and Leopold von Wiese explored the interweaving of actions into large-scale social forms such as the market and the state. A number of these theorists explicitly adopted a terminology of 'points' and 'lines' to depict the networks of connections that tie individuals into the 'knots' and 'webs' of social structure. Wiese (1931) was, perhaps, among the very first to use these quasi-mathematical ideas explicitly in a theoretical monograph, labelling points with letters and referring to the directionality and circularity of interweaving lines of connection.

Sociometry, small groups, and communities

The earliest empirical work on small groups and communities occurred in the United States, where researchers with a background in psychology and psychoanalysis undertook a series of investigations into the friendship choices made in educational contexts by school children and college students. Friendship choices among classmates were seen as a way of exploring the cohesion of school class groups and the relative popularity of particular pupils. Growing out of a long tradition of child study that had peaked with Stanley Hall's (1904) developmental study of adolescence, the earliest published report on friendship networks was that of Helen Bott (1928), who studied play activities among nursery school children.

The leading influence in the development of this work, however, was an Austrian psychoanalyst who had migrated to the United States. Influenced by the way in which Alfred Vierkandt had combined a relational focus with a phenomenological concern for the meanings and emotional significance of relationships, Jacob Moreno devised systematic formal methods for charting social relations among children. Moreno's aim was both to measure and to draw social relations, referring to his work as 'sociometry' and to his drawings as 'sociograms' (Moreno 1934).

Moreno observed children's interaction and counted the numbers of friendship choices made and received by different class members, combining these into sociograms that depicted each child as a point and their friendship choices as lines with arrow heads. These arrow heads showed the direction in which a choice was made: distinguishing 'outgoing' choices directed *at* others from 'incoming' choices received *from* others. This method allowed Moreno to identify the most popular 'stars' of attraction and the relative 'isolates' who received few or no friendship choices. An example of one of his sociograms is shown in Figure 1. Moreno was also able to see whether certain children attempted to make friends with others but were not able to secure reciprocal choices from those they sought out. Through

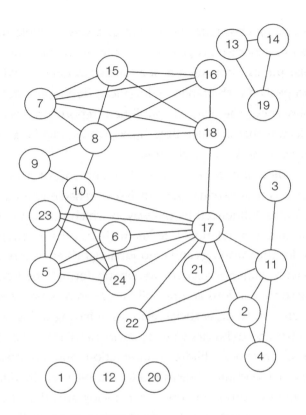

Figure 1 An acquaintanceship sociogram
(Source Moreno 1934: 145)

compiling the various friendship choices made by class members into a single sociogram, Moreno aimed to use a sociometric investigation to model the overall connectedness and emotional climate of the group (see Jennings 1948).

One influence on Moreno's work was the tradition of *Gestalt* psychology. Kurt Lewin, also a German émigré to the United

States, was even more firmly embedded in this tradition of analysis and pioneered a more general psychology of small groups. *Gestalt* psychology involves a focus on the mental structures that allow people to organise and make sense of their experiences, basing its ideas on observations of non-human primates (see Köhler 1917). Lewin aimed to translate this basic idea to the social level, aiming to show that the social structures of groups are the means through which their actions are organised and constrained. His investigations into social groups were concerned, then, with how such structures are produced and the effects they have on the communication and actions of their members.

Lewin's starting point was to see groups as 'fields' of interaction—hence his adoption of the term 'field theory' to describe his approach. A group field is the life space within which people act, and their friendship choices and other social relations are to be understood as creating forces of attraction and repulsion within the field that constrain the flow of ideas through the group. A particular individual, for example, is able to communicate ideas only through his or her direct contacts or through intermediaries who are able to pass them on. The diffusion of ideas, then, depends upon the structure of group relations within which the communicating individuals are located.

The work of Lewin inspired a series of experimental studies that led to the establishment of 'group dynamics' as a specialism within social psychology (Cartwright and Zander 1953; Harary and Norman 1953). It was in this specialism that researchers began to use more systematic mathematical arguments to model group structure. Using the mathematical approach called graph theory, which investigates the formal properties of networks, or 'graphs', of all kinds, they began to operationalize ideas of the 'density' of sociograms and the 'centrality' of individuals. In graph theory, the formal properties of points and lines in a network become the objects of a mathematical analysis that discloses the constraints that shape network form.

Researchers in group dynamics constructed formal models of group structure, such as the star, the 'Y', the chain, and the circle (see Figure 2), and held that these structures had very different implications for effective communication because some individuals are in critical 'central' positions. If a group is structured into a long chain of connections in which information is communicated by passing it through a series of intermediaries, then it is likely that meanings will become slightly distorted and altered with each step in the flow of communication. Much as happens in the children's game of Chinese Whispers, the message received at the end of the chain may be quite different from that sent at the beginning. In a group in which there are many direct connections and alternative channels of communication, on the other hand, meanings are less likely to alter as they flow through the group because the multiple channels introduce 'corrections' and so greater conformity in thought and behaviour is to be expected.

Intermediaries in social groups, especially those at the centres of 'stars', have been seen as the potentially more powerful members of their groups: they are the influential opinion leaders because of their central locations within the group. Research in group dynamics has explored the ways in which relations of dependence within groups can enhance or diminish power and

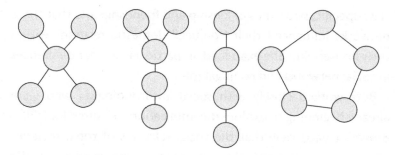

Figure 2 Sociometric structures: star, Y, chain, circle

foster particular structures of leadership (French and Raven 1959). Other investigators have focused rather more on the extent to which social relations are reciprocated and, therefore, the patterns of 'balance' and imbalance that characterise different groups (Davis 1963). The research of Festinger (1957) linked this with ideas of subjective mental balance in attitudes and ideas so as to explore particular patterns of group response (Festinger *et al.* 1956).

In the 1930s, George Lundberg (1936; Lundberg and Steele 1938) had extended basic sociometric techniques to the study of village communities, but it was not until the 1950s that sociometric techniques really began to move beyond small and experimental groups to larger groups in real settings. The Canadian social psychologist Elizabeth Bott—daughter of the pioneering sociometric researcher Helen Bott—worked at the Tavistock Institute, where sociometry and group dynamics had its British base. Here she carried out a comparative study of working-class and middle-class couples in London. Bott (1957) showed that members of each class were embedded in different, class-specific, structures of kinship and friendship and that these networks influenced their 'conjugal' domestic relations within their households. She examined, in particular, gender differences in social networks and conjugal roles.

Bott worked closely with social anthropologists who were already beginning to explore the implications of Alfred Radcliffe-Brown's (1940) view that the social relations of tribal societies could be investigated through constructing models of the 'structural forms' of these relations. John Barnes (1954) brought these ideas together in his report on the communal structure of the fishing village of Bremnes in western Norway and his work proved particularly influential in the work in Central Africa that Max Marwick was establishing as an offshoot of the Department of Sociology and Social Anthropology at Manchester University. Clyde Mitchell, Scarlett Epstein, Bruce Kapferer, and others worked severally on a series of studies of community and kinship and their effects on gossip and strikes. These studies were brought together in an influential collection that aimed to show the power of graph theory as a model for social relations in complex societies (Mitchell 1969).

From the late 1960s, researchers in the United States took advantage of the advances being made in the use of computers for data analysis and began to apply more systematic and rigorous ideas in their studies of larger community and economic networks. Granovetter (1974) looked at friendship relations as sources of information about job opportunities and developed the influential idea that people acquire the most useful information from their more distant ties. When a job opportunity becomes available locally, information flows quickly and rapidly through the dense and well-connected local networks and everyone tends to acquire the same information. More distant job opportunities, however, come to be known about only by those with generally looser connections beyond their immediate locality. Those with such connections may, therefore, have a distinct advantage in their job search activities as they will have more opportunities than those with only locally dense connections (see Figure 3). Granovetter (1973) described this as the thesis of the strength of weak ties.

Figure 3 Strong and weak ties

Wellman (1979; Wellman and Hogan 2006; see also Fischer 1977; 1982) used social survey methods to collect information on friendship and kinship relations in Toronto, Canada. His aim was to explore whether individuals relied exclusively on local connections or were able to keep in touch with those who had moved away to other parts of the city or country. He was able to examine people's range of immediate social contacts, the frequency and perceived intensity of these ties, and the opportunities provided by the telephone and the car to maintain contacts over extended distances.

Bearden and his colleagues (1975; and see Mizruchi 1982; Mintz and Schwartz 1985) investigated corporate board-level connections in top US companies, while Helmers and his colleagues (1975) undertook a similar study in the Netherlands and rapidly extended this into an international comparison (Stokman *et al.* 1985). This research highlighted the relative 'centrality' of banks and financial companies in corporate networks and the changing relationships between financial and industrial companies in major economies. They documented structures of coordination and communication among large business enterprises and pointed to their effects on economic performance and class cohesion.

Cliques, roles, and matrices

The work of the Manchester anthropologists studying African societies was not the first attempt by social anthropologists to investigate social networks. Lloyd Warner worked in the Durkheimian tradition of Radcliffe-Brown and had undertaken a conventional study of kinship among native Australians before moving to the United States and joining with the psychologist Elton Mayo to undertake an anthropological study of a Chicago factory and its workforce. This pioneering use of anthropological techniques to study 'advanced' societies proved important in generating an alternative to purely sociometric studies.

Industrial psychologists working at the Hawthorne electrical works in Chicago had been undertaking experimental studies on the effects of physical conditions on work satisfaction and output. They had discovered that improving the heating and lighting conditions, allowing rest periods, and other physical alterations to the workplace improved worker morale and led to greater productivity. They were confused to find, however, that similar changes occurred when physical conditions were restored to their original state or even allowed to deteriorate. Uncertain how to interpret these findings, they called on Mayo and Warner to advise them. It was soon concluded that the workers were responding to the experiment itself rather than to the changes in physical conditions. The managers had specially selected a group to study, had located them in an area of the factory separate from other workers, and had, for the first time, seemed to show an interest in their welfare. This phenomenon became known as the 'Hawthorne effect' in experimental studies.

In arriving at these conclusions, Mayo and Warner pursued their own observational and experimental studies in the factory. Of particular importance was their observational study of a wiring room where they observed friendly and hostile interactions, cooperation, and offers of help (Roethlisberger and Dickson 1939). Some of their findings were reported as sociograms, though they seem to have been inspired by the electrical wiring diagrams that abounded in the factory rather than by published sociometric work. Their most important work, however, used tabular or matrix representations to depict the formation of 'cliques'. Presenting observed interactions in a table in which the rows represent individuals and the columns represent the occasions in which they participate, allowed the researchers to identify those individuals who interact frequently and the occasions or circumstances in which they interact. They identified a clique in the wiring room that comprised those who tended to help each other and a set of isolates who found it difficult to get

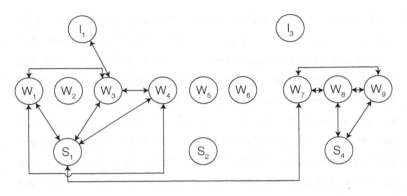

Figure 4 Clique structure
Source: Roethlisberger and Dickson (1939: 507)

help when it was needed and drew this as a diagram (see Figure 4). Cliques were seen as formal representations of the commonly expressed idea that people may feel they are part of an 'in-crowd' or that they are outsiders to it.

Warner decided to pursue similar issues through a community study in the New England town of Newburyport. Regarding this as a typical American town with its roots in the early colonial period, he referred to it as 'Yankee City' in his published studies (Warner and Lunt 1941; 1942; Warner and Srole 1945; Warner and Low 1947; Warner 1963). Later in the 1930s he supervised a similar study in the equally old southern town of Natchez, referring to this as 'Old City' (Davis *et al.* 1941). In these studies, Warner and his teams explored the formation of 'cliques', understood as informal communal groupings based on feelings of intimacy and solidarity and that existed alongside the formal associations of church, business, leisure, and politics. This relationship between communal and associational patterns, informal and formal ties, can be seen in relation to Tönnies (1887) earlier suggestions on the relationship between *Gemeinschaft* and *Gesellschaft*.

The Warner research showed that people tend to be members of numerous overlapping cliques and that it is through the intersection of cliques that overarching structures of community solidarity and cohesion are produced. Warner and his colleagues argued that examination of the pattern of rows and columns in a data table can show the existence of cliques and the relationships among them. Instead of using sociograms, they reported the cliques in Venn diagrams in which circles and ellipses represented sets of interacting individuals, as they had done in the Hawthorne studies (see Figure 5). At an aggregate level for the whole community they allocated individuals to a social class and then represented each social class as a row in a matrix of connections among the various cliques. This procedure allowed them to identify the macro-structural positions found in the communities. Their research highlighted social divisions of both class and ethnicity, showing the existence of a rigid 'colour line' separating black and white communities.

Figure 5 Overlapping cliques in a social hierarchy

George Homans (1950) undertook a systematic review of small-group studies, aiming at a theoretical synthesis of ideas. At the heart of this synthesis was his use of sociometric ideas of the frequency and direction of social relations, but he also explored the matrix methods used by Warner for clique identification. Revisiting the analyses of informal interaction undertaken in Natchez by Warner's team, he began to develop a systematic method of matrix analysis that has since become a central part of social network analysis. Homans looked at the meetings of 18 women at 14 social events, as represented in an 18 × 14 matrix, and claimed that a simultaneous manual rearrangement of rows and columns could bring out the internal clique structure. A matrix is typically arranged in an arbitrary order, listing individuals and events alphabetically or, at best, chronologically. Shuffling the order of rows and columns until a strong pattern appears in the cells discloses the structure that is hidden by these arbitrary arrangements.

This kind of trial and error rearrangement is slow and cumbersome, even for a relatively small group, and Homans's method was not pursued until much later. It did, however, point the way towards systematic investigations of structural positions within networks of the kind that were being suggested by the social anthropologist Nadel (1957). Aiming at a formal, mathematical approach to anthropology, Nadel showed that algebraic methods for set analysis could be used to model the 'roles' within a social structure. Where sociometric uses of graph theory focused on the actual interactions of particular individuals, algebraic set theories focused on the positions and roles that these individuals occupied and at role relations at the level of the social structure as a whole.

Algebraic and matrix methods were developed by Harrison White and others (1963; Lorrain and White 1971) and they were able to take advantage of advances in computing to undertake matrix rearrangements for large-scale social networks. In an approach that they called 'blockmodelling', they saw blocks of cells in a matrix as representing the structural positions that Nadel had sought (White *et al.* 1976; Boorman and White 1976). The individuals who occupy each position are 'structurally equivalent' to each other: they are, for network purposes, interchangeable, and their individual characteristics and connections can be disregarded. Thus, all fathers may be expected to relate in similar ways towards their sons and daughters, while all teachers may be expected to relate in similar ways towards pupils. The characteristics of roles are social facts that are independent of the particular attitudes and outlooks of their individual occupants.

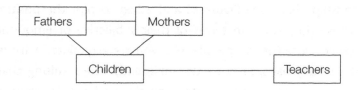

Figure 6 Blockmodel role structure

Space and distance

The sociometric uses of graph theory measured the 'distance' from one individual to another by the number of links that must be traversed to connect the two. This is a useful measure of closeness, but it does not correspond to the everyday idea of distance as something measured across a physical space. In a sociogram, the physical arrangement of points is arbitrary, limited only by the aesthetic attempt to minimise overlaps among the lines. A measure of physical distance, however, requires a non-arbitrary representation of the data. The distance between two towns in miles, for example, can be measured 'as the crow flies' rather than by traversing a network of roads (of varying length) and intersections. A number of network researchers have, therefore, attempted to construct models of 'social space' in which straight line, 'crow flies' distances can be measured (Bogardus 1925; 1959). Embedding a network of connections in such a space allows both the pattern of connections and relative distances to be studied.

In some applications, a simple idea of perceived social distance has been used. Individuals may be presented with a simple friendship chart (see Figure 6) and asked to plot the position of those they know in terms of their subjective or emotional distance: close friends, people who you are acquainted with on a day-to-day basis, or more distant friends. The resulting chart gives a visual representation of a person's social world in terms of the degree of intimacy they have with various numbers of other people (Wallman 1984: 61, 66–7; Spencer and Pahl 2006). These charts have provided a useful approach to affective personal networks.

A more formal idea of social space was inherent in the early work of Lewin, but it really developed as a formal method in psychology. Psychometric studies of attitudes had used methods of 'scaling' to show the relative strength of attitudes and this led

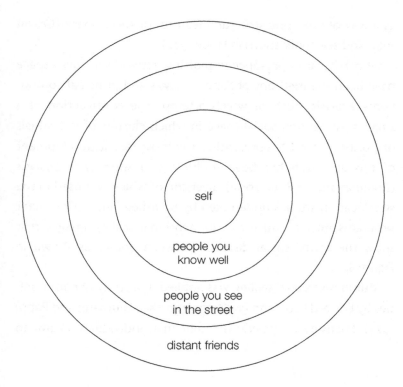

self

people you
know well

people you see
in the street

distant friends

Figure 7 Affective distance in friendship

to attempts to measure two or more attitudes through the intersection of their scales in a cognitive space that could be taken to
represent a structural part of the mind. Such approaches were
called smallest space analysis (SSA) because they involved an
attempt to define the smallest number of dimensions (scales)
that would represent a particular cluster of attitudes. This
approach was generalised as multidimensional scaling (Kruskal
and Wish 1978) and began to be applied to social phenomena

as a way of reporting structural features of social space (Coxon 1982; and see applications in Hope 1972).

Of particular importance in plotting networks in social space have been the methods of factor analysis and principal components analysis, both of which attempt the construction of a smallest-dimension social space in which clusters of individuals or positions can be represented. The most recent development of this approach has been multiple correspondence analysis (Rouanet and Le Roux 2009), a version of which was used in the stratification studies undertaken by Bourdieu (1979). Computer programs now produce multidimensional scaling images that show the actual social distance between points, as shown in Figure 8.

Multidimensional scaling was applied in a study of communities by Edward Laumann (1966; 1973; and see Laumann and Pappi 1976). Focusing on positions rather than individuals, Laumann

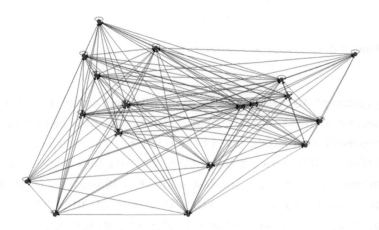

Figure 8 Multidimensional scaling of a network

traced the friendship patterns of those in particular occupational categories. The frequency of friendship ties among pairs of positions was taken as a measure of the distance between the positions and computerised techniques were used to generate an overall space in which the classes could be mapped according to their friendship distance. This was, therefore, an attempt to measure differential association among social classes. Laumann's study generated a three-dimensional model of community structure in which the same social classes could be represented as clouds or clusters of points.

One of the most influential studies that used multidimensional scaling was that of Joel Levine (1972) on interlocking corporate directorships. Using data on large US banks in 1966, Levine constructed measures of similarities in patterns of connection around each of the principal banks. He subsequently used this method to produce a comprehensive 'atlas' of corporate connections (Levine 1984).

Advances in computer software have made it very easy to carry out multidimensional scaling. One of the leading software programs (PAJEK) uses a spring-embedding technique to position a network in a multidimensional space and allows the network to be rotated for the visual inspection of its structure.

Dynamics and social change

The majority of the early studies of social networks have been static and descriptive. They have reported on the features of social networks as they exist at a particular time, but they have not generally attempted to explore the internal dynamics that lead a network to change from one state to another. Where a concern for time and change has been apparent, this has involved the construction of a series of cross-sectional studies with processes of change imputed but not directly studied (see Scott and Griff 1984; Scott and Hughes 1980). A move towards dynamic models is a relatively recent phenomenon and has come about through work by physicists who have been unaware of previous research by social psychologists, social anthropologists, and sociologists.

Motivated by an apparent decline in fundamental theoretical problems in physics itself, a number of physicists have explored the possible extensions of mathematical models from physics to other intellectual fields. Barabási (2002) has been the leading advocate of the application of physical models to social and economic phenomena, seeing himself as a pioneer in virgin territory (Scott 2011b). Highlighting the importance of a paper by Watts and Strogatz (1998), Barabási has produced an approach that, for all its numerous limitations, does provide some novel ideas that have helped to bring about a greater awareness of the importance of dynamic analysis.

Work in this area has used Stanley Milgram's (1967; Travers and Milgram 1969) studies of 'small worlds' to explore the limits to certain kinds of variation in network structure. Milgram was interested in the fact that strangers are often able to identify mutual acquaintances or connections and will exclaim 'what a small world!' To explore this phenomenon he carried out an experiment in which he asked volunteers to pass a message to a named, but unknown, individual in another country. The volunteers were instructed that they must pass the message only to a person known to them and that this second person must also pass the message to a known individual. The message must, therefore, be passed forward in the manner of a chain letter. Each person who receives the message is instructed, however, to pass it on to an acquaintance who they feel is likely to be able to get the message, directly or indirectly, to the target individual. Milgram found that messages could typically get from source to target through an average of six connections, or five intermediate individuals. This is the now-famous idea of 'six degrees of connection'.

Watts and Strogatz began to explore the mathematical properties of the networks in which these experimental conclusions hold. They showed that only certain kinds of networks have these small-world properties and that many of the measures used in social network analysis depended on their presence in the networks studied. Their focus of interest was, therefore, on variations in network structure and shifts of state from a small-world network to either more or less densely connected networks. Duncan Watts (1999; 2003) has shown that small-world properties exist in networks that are clustered into zones of relatively high density and by a differentiation between strong and weak ties. In such a network, the overlapping of connections is so great that the line distances between points are optimally low. A small-world graph contains many 'redundant' links such that points tend to be connected through multiple alternative paths. Watts showed that small changes in the connectivity of such networks can significantly alter their properties if these changes occur close to the threshold levels that define the small-world conditions.

Radical structural changes can therefore follow from minor local-level changes.

Structural change, then, is seen as resulting from the local-level making and breaking of connections and occurs as an unintended consequence of those actions. These kinds of change have been modelled in agent-based computational models that aim to simulate agent decision making and so to trace change over time. This work developed independently of work by physicists (see Snijders *et al.* 2010) but has rapidly been recognised as providing an essential element in the dynamic models proposed by the physicists. Tom Snijders's model depicts individuals as rule followers who make or break their social relations according to particular decision rules. Individuals act 'myopically', without awareness of the larger consequences of their actions (which are, typically, unknown and unpredictable to them). Individuals acting in this way produce incremental linear changes in the overall structure of the network. When their actions reduce the number of redundant links beyond a certain point, however, change may be radical and non-linear. At critical threshold points there is what Watts has called a 'phase transition' that disrupts the capacity of the network to continue developing as before. The diffusion of innovations and the flow of capital, for example, may be completely disrupted by such a transition. When local-level actions increase the number of redundant links beyond an upper threshold point, on the other hand, the network becomes so highly connected that ideas and resources can rapidly spread through the network at such a rate that all positional advantages are lost.

I have reviewed the history of social network analysis through tracing developments in relation to a number of specific methodological approaches. The earliest of these was graph theory and the associated techniques of sociometry. This provides an intuitive modelling of social networks and allows a number of fundamental and advanced measures of network organisation to be calculated. The second mathematical approach I considered was the algebraic use of sets and matrices to uncover the structure of positions and roles within a network. While this approach is perfectly compatible with graph theory, it highlights quite distinct sets of issues. Next I looked at spatial models that emulate geographical mapping techniques to produce spatial configurations of points. These techniques allow a move away from the arbitrary configurations of sociometric sociograms and towards more visually meaningful arrange-ments. Finally, I considered some novel approaches to network dynamics that make it possible to build on the static models of graph theory, matrix algebra, and multidimensional scaling and to construct accounts of structural change and network development. In the chapter that follows, I will introduce the key concepts employed in these approaches, and in Chapter 4 I will look in more detail at some of the applications of those concepts in substantive studies.

Further reading

Scott, John 2012. *Social Network Analysis*. Third Edition. London: Sage. Chapter 2 gives a fuller account of the history of social network analysis.

Prell, Christina 2012. *Social Network Analysis: History, Theory and Methodology*. London: Sage. Chapter 3 provides an alternative account of this same history.

Freeman, Linton C. 2004. *The Development of Social Network Analysis: A Study in the Sociology of Science*. Vancouver: Empirical Press. The definitive and standard full-length history of social network analysis.

Bott, Elizabeth 1957. *Family and Social Network*. London: Tavistock Publications. A good example of a classic early study using network ideas.

Fischer, Claude S. 1982. *To Dwell Among Friends: Personal Networks in Town and City*. Chicago: University of Chicago Press. A more advanced middle-period study of personal networks.

3 Key concepts and measures

Chapter 2 traced the history of social network analysis through the three broad mathematical approaches that have dominated the field: graph theory, algebraic approaches and spatial approaches. In this chapter I will first consider the principal methods of data collection for social network analysis, and I will then outline and define, in sequence, the key concepts and measures associated with each mathematical approach considered in Chapter 2. I will suggest that graph theory provides the formal framework common to all these approaches. I will not present highly technical definitions, as these are more appropriate to the various handbooks of social network analysis (Scott 2012; Degenne and Forsé 1994; Prell 2012). Having done this, I will set out some of the statistical procedures used in assessing the validity of network measures in actual situations.

Collecting network data

Relational data for social network analysis can be collected through a variety of methods. These include asking questions about the choice of friends, observing patterns of interaction, and compiling information on organisational memberships from printed directories. All such methods require that an appropriate selection of cases be made from the total range of possible data sources. In many studies this will involve a complete, or near-complete, enumeration of a whole population. For example, an investigation into the interlocking directorships within the 'top 200' companies in an economy will typically involve the collection of data on all 200 companies. Similarly, an investigation into the friendship patterns of the children in a school class will wish to collect information on all the children in the chosen class.

This emphasis on complete enumeration reflects, in part, the small size of the groups involved and the relative ease with which complete data can be collected. More importantly, however, it reflects the difficulty of using sampling techniques with relational data. Many concepts and measures in social network analysis, as will be seen, require the use of complete data on all network linkages, and only a relatively few measures relating to individuals can be assessed from sampled data. In general it can be said that individual-level or ego-centric measures can be generated from sample data, but that macro-level, structural measures can be produced only with considerable difficulty and uncertainty, or perhaps not at all. While this difficulty is not absolute, it is a major limitation and much research is currently being undertaken to find ways of making more reliable inferences from sample data on social networks.

Once relational data have been acquired, they can be prepared for use in social network analysis. In the case of very small networks, this will generally involve purely manual methods as the analyst can easily keep track of the various individuals and organisations involved. Even where the number of cases reaches 20 or 30, manual analysis of the data may still be possible. In the case of large networks, however, analysis by computer will generally be necessary and the data will need to be stored within the formatted files of the particular software that is to be used.

Data must be sorted on a case-by-case basis, as each case will be represented by a 'point' in the sociograms and the network analyses. Typically, each point and its connections are listed as a numbered row in a data file. For example, each individual may be listed with the organisations or meetings in which he or she is involved. Each such point can be given an identifying reference label, perhaps the name of the individual or an abbreviated form of this, and the label can be stored as part of the row or in a linked file. The various organisations or meetings in which the individuals are involved will also need to be given a label so that this can be married up with the individual data. In some analyses, an investigator will be concerned with the connections among the cases themselves: for example, with the connections among individuals who are involved with the same organisations. In these situations, the rows in the file will need to list the other individuals to which each individual is connected, and this kind of file can easily be generated from the original list by the standard software programs.

Such a data file might show, for example, eighteen women and their participation in a number of social events. Each woman would be represented by a row in the file, and the row would show the particular events that she has attended. From this initial file it is possible to produce a file listing the women and the others who they meet at the various events, and also a file listing the various events that are similar because the same women attend them. Similarly, a file for the analysis of interlocking directorships would show each company as a row, with the rows listing the directors of the company. From this can be produced listings of individuals and their meetings with each other and of companies and their board-level connections to each other. A file showing the friendship choices of schoolchildren would typically record the connections among the children directly, each row showing the other children that are chosen as friends.

Standard social network analysis packages can read these so-called linked lists and can convert them into the various other files that are required for specialist analyses. This normally occurs behind the scenes with there being little or no need for the investigator to directly manipulate the files. It is to the particular concepts and measures available in these packages that I now turn.

Graph theory and egocentric measures

True to its origins in sociometry, uses of graph theory tend to employ the language of points and lines to describe the patterns of connection in a social structure. Its various concepts and measures aim to convey the properties of the visual image of a sociogram. Visualisation is difficult for large and complex networks, but the visual imagery behind the basic concepts of graph theory can help us to imagine the more complex structures of which they are the building blocks. Sociograms are arbitrary aesthetic representations that maintain only the patterns of connections and not any information about physical distance and relative location. The mathematical language of graph theory is, similarly, an attempt to grasp and summarize merely the pattern of connections.

In the simplest cases, any particular point can be connected to any or all of the other points by single lines. The total number of lines connecting an individual is termed the 'degree' of the corresponding point. Where the lines represent, say, relations that result from the presence of two people at the same event or their shared membership of an organisation, the lines are said to be undirected. However, not all social relations are of this simple type. Where friendship choices are being analysed, for example, choices may not be reciprocated and so the 'direction' of the line needs to be considered. Thus, choosing a friend can be seen as a line directed outwardly from the individual making the choice to the person chosen. Similarly, the receiving of a friendship choice from another can be seen as an inwardly directed line. A graph containing directed lines is technically termed a digraph.

Of course, social relations may not all be equally salient, and it is often necessary to have some measure of the intensity or value of the lines. Thus, identifying someone as a 'close friend' involves greater subjective feelings of emotional intimacy than is the case for a 'distant friend' or an 'acquaintance'. It is conventional to assign a numerical value to a line in order to represent the intensity of the relationship, producing a valued graph. Any such numerical value is likely to be arbitrary, being based on the analyst's best guess at the strength of the relationship. Typically, intensity has been measured on an arbitrary 1 to 9 scale, with a value of 9 representing the most intense relationship. One particularly important measure of value is the 'multiplicity' of the line. This is a measure that recognises that two people who are each members of three organisations may need to be represented by a line with multiplicity 3, meaning that they have a closer or more intense relationship than two people with only one organisational membership in common.

The discussion so far has assumed that social relations are positive: that people like each other or find their common organisational memberships significant. However, many social relations are negative or involve hostile attitudes: people dislike each other, reject friendship choices, and so on. Where it is important to distinguish positive and negative relations in a network, a mathematical sign (+ or −) may be attached to the line and the resulting graph is called a signed graph.

These basic concepts of direction, value, and sign allow a mapping of the myriad ways in which individuals and organisations relate to each other. They grasp the basic qualities of interpersonal relations and the more abstract features of macro-structural relations. The most fundamental measures are the so-called egocentric measures that are based on a particular focal individual or organisation, referred to as 'ego'. An individual's immediate friendship choices can be represented as a number of outgoing lines, the size of a person's friendship set being measured by the number of lines—technically referred to as the 'outdegree' of the point. In the same way, friendship choices received are represented and measured by the 'indegree'. Relations of hostility can be measured as the negative outdegree, and all these relations can be regarded as varying in the strength or intensity of the measured lines. Thus, an individual's immediate field of interaction—his or her 'neighbourhood'—can be fully charted with the basic concepts of graph theory.

Not all of the relationships of an individual or organisation are immediate or direct. Some social relations are indirect, involving intermediary points. For example, an individual may not know a particular other, but may 'know a man that does'. Thus two individuals may be indirectly connected through one or more common neighbours. In the words of an old song, a young debutante may sing that she has danced with a man, who danced with a girl, who danced with the Prince of Wales. Such relationships are more distant than are direct relations, and graph theory uses measures of 'distance' to represent this. As I have already noted, this measure departs from the assumptions of spatial distance and is calculated by the number of lines needed to connect two points. Ego is connected to others at varying distances according to the number of lines that run between them. A friend of a friend is connected by two lines and so is said to be at distance 2 from ego. Thus, the singer of the song was connected to the Prince of Wales at distance 3. Distances greater than 2 typically lose their significance for the focal individual very rapidly, and such egocentric measures need to be used with care. Nevertheless, it can be important to know, for example, the size of a person's neighbourhood at distance 2, as this will include a number of potential intermediaries who can connect them to new contacts or sources of information. This was the basis of Granovetter's (1973) important argument about the strength or importance of relations through relatively distant acquaintances.

It is important, of course, to take account of the direction, sign, and value of lines in measuring distance. If the lines connecting two individuals vary in direction, it may make no sense at all to measure the overall distance by the number of lines. Similarly, if the sign of a second line is the opposite of the sign of the first, then the intermediate point may be a barrier to communication rather than a facilitator of it. Finally, lines of high value may, other things being equal, bring points 'closer' together than lines of low value. These remarks highlight the fact that the properties of a social network can never be inferred simply from the mathematical measures that it is possible to make. It is always necessary to ensure that the measure can be given a substantive sociological significance. A connection at distance 2 can easily be given such an interpretation, but a connection at, say, distance 10 may not be at all significant for the individuals or organisations concerned. Such judgements of significance will vary from one type of relationship to another. Distance in a network of friendship may be more significant than, say, distance in a network of credit relations, though this may not always be the case. Thus, a distant and apparently trivial link held in the computer of a credit-rating agency may affect an individual's credit rating quite significantly. The interpretation of any distance measure depends on the expert judgement of the analyst and the purposes of the research.

The last of the egocentric measures to be reviewed here is the neighbourhood density. This is a measure of the extent to which the immediate contacts of a point are mutually connected with each other. Density is what Bott (1957) referred to as the 'connectedness' of a person's network and is high whenever, for example, many of a person's friends are also friends of each other. In an egocentric network with lower density, a person's various friendships are more segmented. For example, if four people are all directly connected to each other, rather than being connected only through the focal ego, then ego's neighbourhood has a density of 100 per cent. This measure of density is more typically represented on a scale of 0 to 1, with complete 100 per cent density being represented as a value of 1. Many of the qualifications entered about line distance apply to the calculations of neighbourhood density, especially where neighbourhoods are defined at line distances of two or greater. Even in the simpler case, however, it is important to take account of the direction, sign, and value of lines in measuring and interpreting density. Other issues in the measurement of density will be discussed later in this chapter.

Graph theory and global measures

While egocentric measures are always focused on a particular point—ego—the overall, or global properties of a network can also be assessed. The connections of particular individuals concatenate to produce a more or less cohesive structure of relations that is unlikely to have been intended by any of the participants. Graph theory provides a set of concepts for analysing these macro-level properties of social networks.

In order to measure global properties, however, it is not generally possible to rely on sample data. The egocentric network properties of a large number of individuals can be measured from a sample survey so long as all the normal issues of representativeness are considered. In the case of most global properties, however, the very act of sampling will result in a loss of the information that is required. Global properties are not mere aggregates or averages, as is usually the case in sample data, but are themselves structural features that are apparent only if a whole network is studied and not simply a sample drawn from it. This is not true for all global measures, and work is currently going on to find a solution to this problem. However, this is an issue that always needs to be borne in mind when seeking to measure global properties.

The most fundamental global properties of graphs are degree-based measures. The idea of line distance, for example, is an important global measure and may be more useful at the global level than it is in egocentric networks. The various lines connecting two points form a 'path' whose length can be defined by the number of constituent lines that chain together to form it. Movement through a network depends importantly on the path distances involved. Thus, the communication of ideas or innovations may occur through a whole chain of intermediaries with little or no reliance on the participants all having direct personal knowledge of each other. This was the key to Milgram's discussion of the 'small world'. Some studies of the diffusion of information have suggested that information degrades with distance simply because each intermediary has less contextual knowledge about the original act of communication and so may misinterpret or distort the information. This is the problem alluded to in the game of Chinese whispers.

Measures of path distance must, of course, take account of the directionality, sign, and value of the various lines. The latter is particularly important as it has been seen as a crucial determinant of the efficiency of the network flow and movement and so as reinforcing any degradation or attenuation effects. A network in which the strength of lines is constant or increasing across paths might be expected, other things being equal, to be an efficient network for communicating ideas or transmitting financial resources. A network in which path distances involve a decline in value at successive steps might be expected to be far less efficient and to result in a significant attenuation of meanings and ideas with distance.

A whole collection of global measures cluster around the idea of the centrality of points within their graphs. The degree of a point—its total of incoming and outgoing lines—is the most basic measure and has been termed local centrality. Calculating the degrees of all points in a network and ranking them from highest to lowest gives a rank order of local centrality. This centrality is 'local' because it highlights points that are well-connected in their immediate neighbourhoods. Such points may not, however, be central in the more global sense that a circle or sphere has a unique centre that can be understood in quasi-spatial terms. Locally central points are well-connected within particular parts of the network but may not be at all well-connected in a global sense.

It is for this reason that a distance-based measure of 'closeness' has generally been preferred as a measure of global centrality. The most commonly used measure of closeness involves calculating the aggregate distances from each point to all others. The score for any particular point is a measure of how close or distant the point is likely to be to any randomly chosen point. The point with the lowest aggregate distance is the most central point in the network. It will be apparent that all the usual qualifications apply and that closeness must be calculated with respect to appropriate indicators of direction, sign, and value.

The converse of centrality is peripherality and it can be useful to know those points that are least close to other members of their networks. Such points are not isolated but are poorly integrated into their network. They are likely to have little influence and to be uninvolved in significant communication flows through the network.

A final measure of centrality is one that measures the extent to which a point is able to act as an intermediary in a large number of network flows. This measure has been called 'betweenness' and refers to the extent to which a particular point is able to serve as an intermediate point of contact between any two other points. The person represented by such a point may be able to control access or the flow of information to others because of the 'structural hole' (Burt 1992) that exists between the two others that he or she connects. A point has a high betweenness centrality when it fills a large number of structural holes in the network. A point with high betweenness centrality may not be at all central in terms of its local degree or global closeness, yet it may play an important part in the structure of the network.

A further set of global measures involve a move away from the properties of points to the properties of the network as a whole. These measures comprise the inclusiveness, density, and centralisation of the network.

Inclusiveness simply measures the number or proportion of the whole set of points that are actually connected into one or more parts of the graph. Some points may be isolates, having no ties to other points, while others will be connected, to a greater or lesser extent, into larger structures. The inclusiveness of a graph is simply the total number of non-isolated points, generally expressed as a percentage of the total number of points. Inclusiveness is a rough and ready approximation to cohesion, but it is usually more informative to measure the actual density of the graph. The idea of neighbourhood density has already been introduced and so the global density of a network should be easy to understand. Global density is the actual number of lines connecting the points of a graph (directly related to inclusiveness) expressed as a proportion of the total number of lines that could possibly exist among the points. Thus, the existence of a large number of isolates reduces the density of a graph. Density can be calculated for valued and directed lines as well as for lines in an undirected graph.

The density of a graph is a very useful and direct measure of its cohesion, but it has one major limitation as a comparative measure of social structure. In real situations, density varies with the size of a network and this limits the possibilities of using the measure to compare different types of network. It is highly unlikely that agents are able to sustain more than a certain number of relationships: our ability to be 'friends' with people, for example, has its limits. Other things being equal, then, an increase in the size of a network is likely to mean a reduction in its density. This is exacerbated by the fact that the ability to sustain relationships varies with the type of relationship. We may, for example, be able to 'recognise' far more people than we would acknowledge as 'friends', and we are likely to 'love' even fewer. A comparison of the density of the recognition, friendship, and love networks, even if they are of a similar size, will therefore be difficult. Nevertheless, for networks of a similar type, the global density can be a useful comparative measure if reported alongside measures of the size and inclusiveness of the graph.

A further measure of global cohesion is the centralisation of a network. Where centrality relates to the position of particular points, centralisation relates to the overall structure of a network. Centralisation measures the extent to which the cohesion of a network is organised around a specific point or set of connected points. The spokes on a bicycle wheel, for example, form a highly centralised network around its hub. Measures of centralisation can be based on the degree, distance, or betweenness of points, and extensions of these concepts have involved the idea that it is possible to identify the sets of points that comprise the centre, margin, and periphery of the network as a whole.

Graph theory and network differentiation

The global measures considered so far are attempts to measure different aspects of the cohesion of a graph understood as its compactness. An alternative strategy is to focus directly on the differentiation or fragmentation of a graph in order to uncover the plurality and diversity of its structure. Such a strategy recognises that connected points in a graph may not be connected as a single whole but may instead be connected into a number of distinct structural parts of the whole network. Two broad approaches to the differentiation of networks into 'subgraphs' can be identified: the measurement of 'components' and the measurement of 'cliques'. Each of these types of subgraph has distinct properties.

A component is a subgraph in which all points are directly or indirectly connected to each other and there are no connections to points outside the subgraph. Information or resources can, therefore, flow along a path through all the members of the component but cannot reach any other points in the graph. A graph may comprise one or more components of varying size, and the number and size distribution of components is a fundamental measure of network differentiation and of the existence of boundaries to the flow of information and resources.

The identification of components must go beyond the simple components of undirected graphs and must take account of any direction attached to lines as this will affect the ability of information or resources to flow from one point to another. In some cases it may be legitimate to disregard direction—for example, in order to measure the 'awareness' of agents choosing friendship partners—and this is what are referred to as 'weak components' in contrast to the 'strong components' in which all points are connected through a path of uniformly directed lines.

A further refinement of the simple component idea is that of the cyclic component built from intersecting cycles of connection. A cycle is a directed path that returns to its starting point. The overlapping of such cycles produces a cyclic component in which all points are connected by one or more cycles and no points have cyclic connections outside the component. A cyclic component is a structural element within a strong component and may be connected to other members of the strong component through 'bridges' that do not lie on the cycle itself.

The various types of component can be further analysed by taking account of degree-based measures such as the intensity or value of the constituent lines. Such an analysis shows the arrangement of components of varying tightness, one inside another. For example, if a measure of value has been attached to the lines, it is possible to slice through the network at various levels of intensity of connection. Such an analysis discloses the 'contour' structure of the network Components of the kind described so far have taken account of all lines, regardless of intensity and so are connected at the lowest level of intensity. If lines below a chosen level of intensity are disregarded, then the higher level of connection is specified and the analysis moves from the 'valley' of the network to its lower slopes. Progressively raising the chosen level of intensity allows the analysis to approach the 'peaks' of the structure, with intermediate levels marking the gradient of the network. Where points are connected at varying levels of multiplicity, this multiplicity can be used to generate a picture of the 'nested' structure. Nested components, then, stack inside each other like Russian dolls.

The other approach to differentiation that I referred to involves the identification of cliques. A clique differs from a component in that it is a set of points in which each point is directly and reciprocally connected to all other points. It represents, for example, a tight friendship group or gang. The definition of a clique is, therefore, far more restrictive than that of a component, and cliques tend to be smaller subsets within components. By taking account of the direction of the lines in a clique, it will be possible to identify strong and weak cliques, and if the values of the lines are taken into account it may even be possible to identify a nested structure of cliques.

This idea of the clique is clear and readily interpretable, but it is relatively unusual to find such a structure in real social networks, except in those with exceptionally high density. For this reason, social network analysts have generalised the idea into that of the '*n*-clique' in which less restrictive conditions apply. This '*n*' is the criterion of connectedness in the clique and so altering the value of '*n*' allows the identification of looser cliques. In a 2-clique, for example, all members are connected at distance 2 or less: each point is either directly connected to all others or is connected through an intermediary point. Such a concept can be seen as representing social groups such as those in which individuals are either friends or friends of friends. Although values of '*n*' greater than 2 can be used in clique analysis, they can less readily be given a substantive sociological interpretation and so may be less useful.

Various extensions of the clique idea have been suggested, though they have, so far, been less widely used in sociological work. The most important of these extensions are the 'clan', in which all points are connected by a path of a specified maximum length, and the *k*-plex, in which all points are adjacent to a specified number of other points. All such measures are available within the principal network analysis programs, but great care must be taken to show that they designate meaningful sociological concepts before they are used.

A final and more useful extension of the clique idea is that of the social circle, seen as a set of overlapping and intersecting cliques (Alba and Kadushin 1976). This concept points to the importance of chains of indirect connections in tying individuals into larger structural elements. The idea of the social circle comes close to the informal idea of the clique originally identified by Warner and his colleagues in their community studies.

Algebraic measures of network structure

Algebraic methods represent the points of a graph in sets that correspond to social 'positions' and that can be handled in equations or analysed in matrices. I have traced the origins of this approach to social network analysis in the works of Warner and Homans. The most important recent developments in algebraic network analysis have been those inspired by Harrison White and his work on 'structural equivalence'.

Structurally equivalent points are those that can be regarded as substitutable for each other: they occupy similar structural positions in relation to others, though they may be connected to *different* others. Culturally defined and institutionalised roles—such as father, mother, child, teacher, and so on—are the clearest examples, but the idea also involves purely relational categories such as classes or political factions that generate structural uniformities of experience and action. The approach taken by Lorrain and White (1971) was to represent agents and their affiliations or participations in a matrix and then to simultaneously rearrange both the rows and the columns until blocks of similarly connected points appear. This 'blockmodelling' reduces the structure of the whole graph to a structure of social positions, such as a role set or a class structure.

The rearrangement of a matrix involves one or another form of cluster analysis (Everitt 1974). Methods of cluster analysis combine or separate points according to their similarity, and in White's approach the similarity between two points is measured by the correlation found in their patterns of connection within a graph (White *et al.* 1976; Boorman and White 1976). The method used by White and his colleagues to identify structurally equivalent positions was termed CONCOR and is available within the standard social network analysis software programs. The boundaries of clusters can sometimes be identified visually—as was the case in Homans's reanalysis of the Old City data—but in larger and more complex networks they must be identified from the patterns of high and low density found in the various blocks. Once a repeated cluster analysis has produced a simplified pattern of zero and non-zero blocks of density, a reduced network can be drawn in which non-zero blocks are represented as super-points and zero blocks are represented by the absence of connections. This is referred to as an 'image graph' and has been seen as a delineation of the positional structure of a social network.

An alternative matrix method is that of Doug White and Karl Reitz (1983), which they call regular equivalence. Structural equivalence takes account of direct connections, but regular equivalence takes account of the wider patterns of connection. It looks at similarity of connections at varying specified path lengths. The resulting matrix of similarities can be analysed through similar cluster analytic methods to yield image graphs. This looser measure of substitutability is, arguably, more useful for much social network analysis.

Algebraic methods offer powerful measures for the analysis of social structure (see Pattison 1993), but they are difficult to apply in highly fragmented and differentiated networks. They may be usefully applied *within* components or fully connected graphs, but are impossible to apply *between* components where no connections exist.

Spatial and cartographical approaches

Spatial approaches such as smallest space analysis and multidimensional scaling are attempts to plot points in a spatial field through geometrical methods that allow the construction of sociograms as true 'maps' showing a configuration of points that depicts their relative physical distance and spatial direction as well as retaining information on the familiar path distances and line directions. As with blockmodelling, spatial approaches start out from measures of similarity (or dissimilarity) but use cartographical techniques to produce a best-fit configuration in which the relative similarities among points correspond directly to the relative physical distances that can be shown on paper or a computer screen.

Central to these methods is the search for an appropriate number of dimensions in which to embed the configuration. A maximum of two dimensions can be directly represented on paper, as is the case with an atlas of physical maps showing places in relation to the north/south and east/west dimensions. Computer software, however, allows the depiction of three-dimensional configurations on screen and allows a configuration to be rotated to show the shape and solidity of the networks from various angles. Such representations give clear visual impressions of the density, centralisation, and fragmentation of the networks. It can be difficult to represent more than three dimensions in physical form, and it may be necessary to resort to simplifications such as, on paper, presenting the successive two-dimensional views of a three-dimensional structure.

However many dimensions are used, there is always the question of providing a sociological interpretation of each dimension. It is rarely the case that a configuration will take a directly geographical form and place points in a north/south and east/west two-dimensional space. In social space, dimensions will tend to show scales of economic or political inequality, civic participation, religious affiliation and so on. The key task in spatial analysis of any given configuration is to rotate it in its space in order to yield the most meaningful interpretation of the arrangement of points. Such an interpretation is never given by the method used but must be made and supplied by the analyst.

The configurations produced by these geometrical methods retain the ideas of relative distance and spatial direction that were highlighted in Lewin's work, and they avoid the arbitrariness that is involved in the classic attempts to draw sociograms.

It is also possible to show the lines that connect points within a spatial map, with the length of each line reflecting the 'as-the-crow-flies' distances between points. Path distances, which in basic graph theory simply represent the number of links, become measures of actual spatial distance along the paths that connect the points. Thus, spatial models combine spatial distance with accurate representations of the 'routes' that must be taken in the communication of information or resources through a network. Notions of centrality may also be clear from the patterns of lines, though globally central points may not appear as spatially central to the whole configuration.

It is also possible to represent components, nesting, and structurally equivalent positions within a spatial configuration. Component boundaries can be drawn around its connected points and measures of the value of the constituent lines can be used to draw the nested boundaries within this. Such a diagram corresponds closely to the depictions of hills and valleys on a map by the drawing of contour lines. Such an approach gives a ready depiction of the topography of a social space and can give a useful way of interpreting its structure. Positional ideas may be more difficult to represent with such clarity, as the members of the various blocks may not be spatially contiguous. Nevertheless, the use of different colours to represent the various blocks will bring out the equivalence patterns and so help to identify the relationships between block membership and the membership of cliques and components.

These uses of spatial analysis have been made possible by advances in computing. These have allowed the handling of large data sets and the easy and quick production of sociograms, but they have also allowed the use of powerful on-screen methods for visualising the social networks generated. Standard software allows the inspection of three-dimensional configurations and allows the points to be coloured to indicate their properties. More specialised programs allow moving pictures to be constructed so as to depict patterns of change over time.

Statistical inference

Much work in social network analysis has been both static and descriptive. Recent work, however, has shown how it is possible to move towards dynamic understandings of social change and to construct explanations of the patterns described. This has led to much greater attention being given to statistical methods for assessing the significance of results and the validity of explanations. This work follows the general and well-established principles of statistical inference and hypothesis testing, adapting these to the specific requirements of using relational data.

A hypothesis to explain observations must be produced by expert use of the sociological imagination, but any hypothesis proffered must be tested before it can be accepted with any confidence. Statistical methods of hypothesis testing involve comparing the observed results from particular patterns of change to the results that might be expected to occur as a result of random variations alone. That is, the methods attempt to show the likelihood that any result could have occurred simply by chance. If this probability is low, then some confidence can be taken in the mechanisms that have been hypothesised.

A number of approaches to the significance testing of relational data have now been proposed, the most influential and important being the so-called exponential random graph models (ERGM) of Wasserman and his colleagues (see, for example, Wasserman and Pattison 1996; Wasserman 1980). This approach uses regression techniques to compare an observed pattern with a range of possible graphs produced through random simulations from the same data. Confidence in the significance of the observed results is greatest when it corresponds with a randomly generated pattern that has a very low probability of occurrence by chance.

Further discussion of statistical inference is beyond the scope of this book. The method will, however, be of increasing importance in social network analysis, which has constantly been bedevilled by the critical comment: 'So what?'. Critics have pointed to the fact that simply describing an observed configuration of points and lines means nothing unless a plausible sociological interpretation can be given to it. Statistical methods will be an essential element in avoiding this critical response in future.

Further reading

An appropriate working strategy for building on the ideas outlined in this chapter would be to work through the following sources in sequence:

Scott, John 2012. *Social Network Analysis*. Third Edition. London: Sage. The principal chapters in this book cover all the concepts and measures in greater detail and are designed to be read by those with little or no technical background in social network analysis.

Scott, John and Carrington, Peter C. (eds.). 2011. *The Sage Handbook of Social Network Analysis*. London: Sage. A comprehensive collection of introductory material that elaborates on basic concepts with greater background. Section 3 covers key methodological ideas.

Wasserman, Stan and Faust, Katie 1994. *Social Network Analysis: Methods and Applications*. New York: Cambridge University Press. The best and most advanced text that gives a thorough and comprehensive discussion of techniques of social network analysis.

Carrington, Peter J., Scott, John and Wasserman, Stanley (eds.). 2005. *Models and Methods in Social Network Analysis*. Cambridge: Cambridge University Press. A collection of specialised papers reviewing recent advances and leading-edge developments in network methodology.

Background sources on all key areas of network analysis have been brought together in various compilations and source books:

Scott, John (ed.). 2002. *Social Networks*, Four Volumes. London: Routledge. Volumes 1 and 2 include key sources on concepts and techniques.

Holland, P. and Leinhardt, S. (eds.). 1979. *Perspectives on Social Networks*. New York: Academic Press. A shorter collection with a number of important source papers.

4 Applications of network analysis

My outline of the key concepts and measures has, inevitably, been rather abstract and formal. I want now to make these ideas more concrete by illustrating their use in empirical studies that have applied them in relation to substantive sociological issues. I will do this through a consideration of three of the areas that have made the most extensive use of social network analysis. First, I will look at work on the diffusion of ideas and practices through social networks, showing how the structure of a network can shape the flow of information and resources. Secondly, I look at studies of the scholarly networks created through the citation of scientific papers, training at graduate research centres, and participation in scientific conferences and workshops. I will show that these studies have produced mappings of the intellectual space within which scientific production takes place. Thirdly, I will examine studies of corporate power through investigations of interlocking directorships. I will explore issues of centrality and its relation to corporate power and the existence of bank-centred cliques and clusters.

Diffusion and the flow of information and resources

Diffusion studies are concerned with how the flow of information and attitudes about new practices and techniques are shaped by the structures of the networks in which intercommunicating individuals are involved. The earliest writer to highlight the need to investigate diffusion in this way was the French lawyer and criminologist Gabriel Tarde, who saw imitation as the basic psychological mechanism responsible for this diffusion. In his *Laws of Imitation* (Tarde 1890), he set out an account of the factors that constrain imitation and explored the consequences of these for the spread of new ideas and technical innovations. Interaction, he argued, is grounded in the natural tendency for individuals to imitate the behaviour of those who are psychologically close to them and with whom they identify. Thus, interaction is necessarily a process in which individuals behave, intentionally or unintentionally, in ways that those they encounter may either take up or ignore. Innovations made by one individual are, therefore, subject to selective retention and replication, much as genetic variations are selectively replicated in Darwinian theory.

Tarde saw chains of such processes of imitation as the basis on which 'rays' or 'waves' of innovation spread from focal innovators to permeate a whole network. As more and more individuals adopt the innovation, it is able to spread in multiple and intersecting waves that are constrained in their movement by the paths and blockages inherent in a given pattern of social connections. Cultural transmission is not, therefore, a simple and unproblematic process but is complex in both its causation and its consequences. One of Tarde's principal conclusions was that the rate at which an innovation spreads can be described in an 'S' curve in which the number of those who adopt an innovation increases slowly at first but then takes off exponentially until it again slows down at the point where few potential adopters remain. Tarde highlighted the importance of those who are regarded as exemplars or role models. These are the people that individuals look up to and respect and who are especially likely to be imitated. These individuals are the influential 'opinion leaders' in the process of diffusion.

Tarde's suggestions had some influence in studies of political communication and opinion formation, but he had little wider impact until the 1940s. It was then that the full range of his ideas began to be appreciated in a small number of studies in rural sociology. The most important of these studies was that of Ryan and Gross (1943), who studied the release of a strain of hybrid corn to farmers in Iowa. Tracking its adoption from its initial release in 1928, they showed how it eventually revolutionised farming techniques in the State. The hybrid seed was developed by research scientists at Iowa State University and was promoted through the advertising and sales campaigns of the seed companies. Take-up of the corn, however, depended on the massive job of persuading farmers to purchase new seed each year, rather than the traditional practice of relying on a saving of seed corn from the current year's crop. The new seed would be successful only if farmers could be persuaded to make a substantial and continuing investment in the purchase of seed. Successful adoption of the innovation therefore required a significant change in behaviour.

Ryan and Gross showed that the rate of adoption over the period of the study followed the 'S' curve suggested by Tarde. Although sales publicity could make most farmers aware of the new products, there were initially only a small number of early adopters. Most of those who eventually used the new corn did so only after discussion with neighbouring farmers who could persuade them that using the new corn was worthwhile. Persuasion through discussion, rather than simple imitation, was the key to adoption, and people were especially likely to be persuaded by the early adopting opinion leaders whose views they valued. When a number of neighbours had adopted it and advocated its use, other farmers were very likely to take it up. Thus, the initial spread was slow until there were sufficient adoptees for many farmers to have at least one adopter in their neighbourhoods. Take-up then accelerated rapidly as the number of new adopters increased across the State. Eventually, however, a point was reached at which few non-adopting farmers remained and the rate of adoption slowed down.

Only in the 1960s was there any advance on this work. James Coleman and his associates (1966) undertook a study of the introduction of the new antibiotic Tetracycline (referred to in the study as 'Gammanym') and of its adoption by general practitioners. Though unaware of the earlier work of Ryan and Gross, they also discovered both that the pattern of adoption followed an 'S' curve and that the opinion leaders were of key importance in this process. Coleman also found that those with the highest neighbourhood degrees, as measured by hospital affiliation, attendance at staff meetings, and sharing an office with other doctors, were more likely to be early innovators and were most likely to be named as sources of information or as friends by other doctors. These were the people who became early innovators through a 'chain reaction' or contagion effect that ran through their well-connected neighbourhoods. They subsequently became influential contacts working through what Granovetter was to term the 'weak ties' and so were responsible for the spread of the innovation to other parts of the network where local opinion leaders sponsored its take up and influenced others in their area.

A few years earlier than the Coleman study, Everett Rogers (1962) had undertaken a systematic review of research on innovation and had drawn this together into a systematic review of the area. Initially publishing this work in 1963, it took its definitive form in the Third Edition of 1983 and appeared in its Fifth Edition in 2003. Rogers showed that the overall inclusiveness, fragmentation, and density of interpersonal networks determine the extent of exposure people have to new ideas and ways of behaving. The relative location of individuals within this network—their peripherality, the size of their neighbourhood, their involvement in cliques and clusters—determine the extent and salience of their exposure. He highlighted a social process in which there were distinct phases of knowledge, persuasion, and decision: individuals who adopt an innovation must become aware of it, form an attitude towards it, and decide to adopt it.

Rogers argued that individuals are likely to become aware of new ideas that meet their needs or interests as a result of their exposure to the information that flows through a social structure. While people may sometimes actively search out innovations, they are more typically dependent on formal and informal messages that come to them through their regular channels of communication. This is how they may even be made aware of new products and services that they did not previously realise they 'needed'. Those who acquire knowledge early—the 'early knowers'— are those who have a large number of social contacts and a wide sphere of interaction through which they can reach them. Mass media channels are, however, of greatest importance in the knowledge phase of the diffusion process.

Rogers rejected the dubious psychological assumption of a natural propensity to imitate. An idea is taken up only if individuals are persuaded to act on their knowledge: they must develop a favourable attitude towards it through assessing its likely pros and cons. This is most likely to occur when a person is aware that others who he or she have cause to trust are considering it or have already adopted it. The more of a person's contacts that are in this state, the more likely is he or she to form a favourable attitude. It is only at this point that an explicit decision to adopt or not to adopt is made, with collective pressure being especially important in bringing about conformity with the evolving decisions within a person's sphere of contacts. The more people an individual is aware of who have made a decision to adopt, the more likely is he or she to follow suit.

Within this process a key role is played by the opinion leaders that occupy central positions within networks. They are the key determinants of the rate of adoption because their position in their social network makes them critical to the flow of information through it—making them influential for a large number of people—and because their respected status means that their opinions carry a great deal of weight (which can be represented by the intensity of the lines connecting them to others). Thus, diffusion must be studied in relation to the structures of the neighbourhoods in which people are embedded. The three-fold process of knowledge, persuasion, and decision proceeds iteratively and cyclically, such that the critical mass of adopters builds up and larger and larger numbers of individuals are exposed to the pressures that encourage them to adopt an innovation. This explains how the observed exponential shape of the 'S' curve is a direct consequence of this ongoing process.

This approach to innovation has been applied in a number of recent studies. In an investigation of the spread of Christianity, Rodney Stark (1996) asks how it was that a tiny and obscure Messianic movement on the edge of the Roman Empire with a maximum of around 1000 adherents in 40AD was able to dislodge pagan beliefs and grow to more than 33 million adherents by 350AD, the year that the Emperor Constantine converted to Christianity and allowed the religion to become the dominant faith of the western world. The annual growth rate for contemporary religious movements is around 40 per cent and Stark assumed this to be the case for early Christianity. Using this figure, he showed that a constant and realistic annual growth rate does, indeed, produce an exponential absolute growth on the scale suggested by the evidence. The growth of Christianity followed an 'S' curve, with the crucial upturn occurring between 250AD and 300AD.

In order to explain this pattern of growth, Stark drew on the idea of differential association. Conversion to a new religious group, he argued, is more likely when people have stronger attachments to existing members than they do to non-members. It is the balance of attachments rather than doctrinal commitment, that explains the propensity to listen, join, and *then* become committed. Thus, the basis for the growth of a religious movement is to be found in the social networks of direct and intimate interpersonal attachments. Individuals are more likely to respond positively to those with whom they are close and share attitudes and outlook. When recruited, they are especially likely to bring in or ease the recruitment of their immediate family members and intimate associates. Successful religious movements are those that avoid becoming 'closed' and are able to reach outsiders, especially through their weak ties.

Stark showed that early recruitment to Christianity occurred through the networks of the Hellenised Jews, who were already somewhat detached from Palestinian Judaism but were also marginal to Greek society itself. It was through their networks of mutual support and social solidarity that Christianity was able to grow through the Synagogue communities. Thus, conversion in the earliest years was most marked in such cities as Caesarea, Damascus, Antioch, Corinth, Ephesus, and Rome. These were the larger cities of the Graeco-Roman world, many being the diaspora cities of Asia Minor, where Jews constituted a large enough group to form a 'critical mass' for conversion. These cities were, however, relatively disorganised, as they were newly re-established and with colonial and migrant populations. They were also relatively 'open cities' in which many people would have had weak ties to other such cities. It was here that Christianity had its greatest appeal as providing an answer to the prevalence of deprivation and suffering.

Oliver and her colleagues (Oliver *et al.* 1985; 1988b; Oliver *et al.* 1988a; Marwell and Oliver 1993) have developed an approach that extends the standard model of diffusion to the intermittent and cyclical processes that allow the formation or strengthening of social movements and the organisations that carry their ideas forward in concerted joint action and collective protest. Following Roger Gould (1993), they argue that 'closed' organisations—those that are relatively self-contained clusters of related individuals formed into overlapping cliques—can develop and sustain the solidarity required for joint action far better than can 'open' organisations. Thus, a cell structure may be an appropriate organisational form for a radical political group. They show also that the diffusion processes in social movements can generate periodic 'spikes' of activity and a cyclic rise and fall in protest activity, especially where the extent of diffusion is strongly influenced by news media coverage (Oliver and Myers 2003). Gould himself (1995) applied similar ideas in his own study of the formation of popular protest movements in nineteenth century Paris.

These diffusion ideas were brought into the mainstream of formal social network analysis by Ronald Burt (1987; 2005), who connected social influence with analyses of social capital. Tom Valente (1995) has usefully summarised these arguments in a formal extension of Rogers's argument.

Citation studies and the sociology of science

A long tradition of research has outlined the use of publication patterns and, especially, citation patterns, to map forms of social organisation in science. Building on suggestive research into the importance of 'scientific communities' and groups of scientists in the formulation and growth of scientific knowledge (Kuhn 1962; Price 1963), Diana Crane (1972) was one of the first to use ideas from diffusion research to explore scientific innovation, the formation of scientific specialisms, and their basis in processes of recruitment, promotion, and co-authorship. While she used sociometric measures, derived from Coleman's software, she concentrated on diffusion and scientific growth and did not report her findings in what is now standard sociometric format. Nevertheless, she produced a pioneering study that set the baseline for later investigations into scientific networks.

Crane showed that the growth of knowledge within a scientific specialism exhibits the characteristic 'S' curve of diffusion and asked what it is about scientific communities that can explain this. She pursued this question through a study of two specialisms: the rural sociologists concerned with agricultural innovation and mathematical work on finite groups. Authors of published papers in each of these areas were the basis for a mapping of networks of the scientific relations resulting from involvement in informal discussions, published collaborations (co-authorship), relations with teachers, and the influence of colleges on the selection of research problems and methods. Crane found a close correspondence between the structures found in each of these forms of relationship: between two thirds and three quarters of all authors were connected into a large, low density component, and up to a half of the authors reported that they thought these relationships were important in their research. They formed a 'circle', as defined by Kadushin, in that they were loosely bounded structures of communication and awareness whose members are geographically dispersed and so are largely engaged in correspondence, co-publication, and intermittent and infrequent face-to-face discussion. A majority of the members of each specialism were, directly or, more typically, indirectly in contact with a majority of the other members.

Groups of associates were identified on the basis of those who were named as collaborators in scientific projects. These were seen as the 'invisible colleges', the virtual laboratories and work groups through which research is organised. The number of publications produced by an individual was found to be the basis of the longevity of their career as a member of the specialism and of their ability, therefore, to influence norms and practices within it. Isolates and members of small cliques were less likely to be regarded as influential within the specialism. Successful specialisms were those with dominant—central—individuals who acted as the 'leaders' who trained or collaborated with a large proportion of other members. Crane concluded that the peripheral and isolated members of scientific communities must rely on formal mechanisms of communication rather than the informal networks of communication and so are less able to keep up-to-date and are less likely to make significant contributions to their field.

Shortly after Crane's study an exploration into the structure of theoretical debates in American sociology was undertaken by Nicholas Mullins (1973), using somewhat more systematic network methods. Mullins saw theoretical 'schools' of thought as invisible colleges formed from relations of communication, co-authorship, apprenticeship, and colleagueship. A new theoretical orientation, he argued, develops from an initial loose stage in which work is carried out by isolated theorists at a number of different universities, through a 'network stage' in which key publications become the focus of work by people in frequent communication with each other, and a 'cluster stage' in which groups of students and colleagues form around the key specialists in a small number of universities. Finally, a theoretical area may reach the 'speciality stage' in which students who have begun independent careers carry the work to a larger number of institutions and build up their own links to new students and junior co-authors.

Theoretical groups were identified from a reading of the literature and discussion with colleagues, and Mullins undertook separate network analyses for each of the eight areas that he chose to study. Data on training and careers were collected from interviews and from information included in directories, footnotes, and other published sources. Data on co-authorship came from the indices of the *American Journal of Sociology* and the *American Sociological Review*, together with the actual books and articles produced.

Mullins's first report was on what he called 'Standard American Sociology', perhaps the most successful of all theoretical specialisms. This grew from the initial suggestions of Parsons (1937) to become the mainstream of American sociology through the 1950s and 1960s. This entered its network stage in 1935, with a particular focus on Harvard and Columbia, and entered its cluster stage a decade later. Under the intellectual leadership of Parsons, a cluster of 13–15 students, teachers, and researchers forged the central elements of the structural-functional approach. From 1951 it expanded its influence at other universities and established itself as the dominant theoretical orientation in the United States.

Turning to the secondary tradition of symbolic interactionism that emerged at Chicago and reached its specialty stage in 1952, Mullins shows this to be an extensive but somewhat looser network of researchers. The network of co-authorship included five components, the largest including thirty-seven members. Central participants were Ernest Burgess, in the earliest stages, and then Anselm Strauss, Howard Becker, and Everett Hughes. This core group of symbolic interactionists, like two of the smaller components were connected to authors from within the structural functionalist group, and Mullins took this and the fragmentation of the network as indicators of a relatively loose structure.

This structure can be contrasted with ethnomethodology, which emerged around Harold Garfinkel's seminars at UCLA in the mid-1950s, expanded through Berkeley and Santa Barbara, and began a diffusion of influence as a specialism in 1971. The group was much smaller than the structural-functional group and the network of the invisible college was far more fragmented. The co-authorship network, for example, comprised seven components, three of which were simply pairs. The largest component included nine authors and had its focus in Aaron Cicourel, who co-authored with all of the other eight members. Indeed, without Cicourel, the large component would have shrunk to a triad.

A particularly influential use of this approach to intellectual development was Randall Collins's study in *The Sociology of Philosophers* (2000), in which he provided a theoretical rationale for network studies. Collins started out from the assumption that individual thought in philosophy and science can be under-stood as the internalisation and coalescence of ideas circulating through the networks in which scientists and philosophers are involved. An intellectual may work physically alone, as a lone scholar, but always within a social context that means that he or she is never mentally alone. Thus, 'Thinking is a conversation with imaginary audiences' (ibid., 52). Collins therefore argued for the need to study intellectual activity through what have been called the collaborative circles (Farrell 2001) and other networks of association through which cooperation, influence, and argument take place.

This provides the rationale for selecting the particular relations that have been studied in the investigations of the invisible colleges. Ideas are communicated face-to-face in meetings, congresses, lectures, and workshops, through systematic and informal training, and in written texts such as articles, monographs, textbooks, working papers, and so on. Changes in communications technologies supplement these relations with new forms of e-mail and on-line communication. These various networks of linkage are embedded within 'organisational bases' that make communication possible: systems of higher education, publishing, retailing, and professional organisation that sustain their reproduction as an intellectual way of life. Studying such processes over a period of more than two thousand years, from Classical Greece to the present day, involves considerable problems of data consistency and reliability. Collins uses much qualitative and, it must be admitted, impressionistic data, aiming to compile as much source material as possible on intellectual apprenticeship and teaching, publication, recruitment and promotion, and debate, and attempting to document negative, conflict relations as well as the more positive ones. Collins's approach depends upon the *ad hoc* discovery of personal links and on his ability to infer intellectual lineages from his knowledge of the philosophical positions.

Collins's work can best be illustrated by taking his analysis of the period from 1765 to 1935: the period since Kant and in which the universities underwent a radical transition from a patronage system to the contemporary system of research universities (Collins 2000: Chapters 12 and 13). This was the period in which the influence of idealist philosophers who had broken with theological ideas spread with the German model of the university and gave birth to a whole swathe of new philosophies. Collins traces the massively influential links from Kant to his pupil Herder and to his close friend Goethe and then from these to Fichte, who initiated a fully idealist system and was a central figure in influencing Schelling, Schopenhauer, and Hegel. Conflict between Hegel and Schopenhauer followed a split in the network that presaged a decline in the influence of Schopenhauer at the same time as a massive growth in the influence of Hegel. Hegel's influence grew with the prominence of Berlin in the German university system and was the basis for expansion abroad.

In Britain, Collins argues that university reform was marked by the growth of idealism into a philosophical culture hitherto dominated by the utilitarianism of non-professional philosophers. Developing through Jowett, Green, and Bradley at Oxford, it became the dominant approach to philosophy through the interlinked careers of their students Caird, Seth, and Bosanquet. Critical attacks from Bradley on other philosophers fragmented the expanding system into a number of distinct clusters of ideas and individuals: the evolutionary and positivistic thought of Huxley, Lewes, and Eliot, and, through the central position of Russell, the soon-to-be-dominant school of analytical philosophy. The latter included Russell's teacher Whitehead, Moore, Keynes, and members of the tightly knit friendship clique of the Bloomsbury Group, and it influenced the independent line taken by Russell's student Wittgenstein.

Collins's work, then, provides a clear theoretical basis for the use of citation and other data on scientific linkages to map intellectual networks. His own work, inevitably, faced data problems that meant he needed to take a more impressionistic approach to data analysis than had been the case in the studies by Crane and even by Mullins. However, recent work by Howard White has brought such work into the mainstream of social network analysis and established a clear basis for both theoretical and methodological advance.

White and his colleagues (2004) studied the 'Globenet' research group, a pseudonym for a small international and interdisciplinary research group. The researchers aimed to investigate both the social and intellectual structures of the Globenet group and so looked at citation practices among members, together with such social ties as friendship, research contacts, and advice-seeking, and they also undertook some interviews. The core of their analysis, however, concerned citation patterns. Taking four time periods from pre-1989 up to 2000, they looked at the changing patterns of both 'intercitation' (the citation of each other) and of co-citation (joint citation of the same source).

The study found that although three quarters of members did not cite each other, there was a growth in the overall level of intercitation over the whole period. Similarly, the density of the network increased substantially. The distribution of intercitations was found to be scale free, a small number of researchers accounting for a large proportion of all citations. Those who engaged in mutual citation tended to rate each other as 'friends', were involved in direct collaboration, worked in the same discipline, and knew each other from before Globenet was set up. The editors of a collectively produced book were central to the network and also played a leadership role within it. It was found that they had especially high levels of out-citation, showing that they took seriously the need to solidify the group by affirming its collective identity in their own publications.

Co-citation patterns tended to reflect disciplinary differences, though some individuals appeared as 'interdisciplinary linchpins' (White *et al.* 2004: 120). The extent of cross-disciplinary citation increased as the project developed. Intercitation increased with the total amount of scholarly communication and with communication outside of meetings. It correlated with written (and e-mail) communication, but not with telephone use, and it correlated negatively with face-to-face scholarly communication through attendance at the same conferences and workshops.

White and his colleagues concluded that citation patterns reflect both the social structure of the research group and its intellectual consolidation. Over and above the effects of group leadership, people tended to cite each other's work when they were better acquainted with each other. The development of the Globenet project increased the tendency of its members to cite the work of other members. It was also found, however, that there was a tendency for citation to reflect intellectual affinities of theory or method.

The possibilities of using systematic network methods are vividly illustrated in work by Moody and Light (2006), who used citation data to investigate the overall structure of sociology as a discipline within the social sciences. They look at the co-citation of social science journals in order to discover how similar any two journals are in their contents in terms of citations to them by papers in other journals. The raw data on similarities among 1,657 journals were mapped into a multidimensional space and the authors devised a way of drawing contour lines that surround journals with specified levels of similarity. Peaks in the contour map, they argue, can be seen as 'discipline'-specific clusters of journals.

The mapping produced by Moody and Light (2006: 71, Fig 1) shows strong and closely linked clusters for law and economics, closely connected to similar clusters for political science. On the immediately opposite side of the map is the strong cluster of psychology journals. Spread between law and psychology are a series of lower peaks corresponding to management and organisational behaviour. In the opposite direction, the 'foothills' from psychology trail through education and social work. Sociology appeared as a moderately high peak in the dead-centre of the map, while geography and anthropology appeared as low foothills between sociology and political science. The height of the peaks in the Moody and Light map correspond to the sharpness of the boundaries defining a journal's authors, and hence the boundaries of a discipline. Sociology, they found, is not so strongly inwardly influenced as psychology or economics, tending to draw on other disciplines and to contribute to them. By contrast with economics, sociology has no clear structure of central or core journals.

From this mapping of social science, they turn to a detailed mapping of sociology itself, tracing changes in journal connections over the period 1970 to 1990. This time they looked at the topics discussed in articles in order to investigate the state of sociological discourse. Their analysis is, therefore, a conceptual network of journal content based on a frequency count of words. They show that in the 1970s, there were strong clusters for community, education, race, and culture, with each of these surrounded by looser groupings of topics. By the 1990s this had completely changed, with strong areas being health, family, gender, and science-teaching. Sex as a topic of study in sociology journals had grown considerably and was linked to a new large peak of articles on AIDS-HIV. All other areas were much looser than before. Finally, by the late 1990s, the AIDS peak had shrunk back somewhat and was matched by peaks on health care, welfare, language, and stratification, together with interlinked peaks on science, technology, and the sociology of sociology.

Sociology, then, Moody and Light found to be in constant interchange with neighbouring 'stronger' disciplines, and with its specialisms restructuring in relation to trends in the outside world. There is a constant shift in *topics* of study, although the body of sociologists producing these may be more constant and cohesive.

Interlocking directorships and corporate power

Studies on the role of company directors have a long history in social science, though its immediate origins were in journalistic and political investigations of the concentration and abuse of economic power. Directorships have long been seen as sources of power. A directorship in a company, or corporation, is a position at the top of a company that confers legal authority over its assets and employees on its occupant. Holding directorships in two or more companies proportionately increases the power of the individual concerned. Thus, tabulations of the number and distribution of directorships has been seen as a way of charting the degree to which corporate power is concentrated in the hands of a small number of individuals or families.

The earliest studies of this power were those of Otto Jeidels and John Hobson. Jeidels, a member of a Frankfurt banking family who became a leading investment banker and himself the holder of multiple directorships, published a study of board-level relationships between banks and heavy industry in Germany (Jeidels 1905). He tabulated the total numbers of directorships held by directors of each of the big six banks and traced whether these directorships were held by bankers or industrialists and so could be assigned a direction: from banks to industry or *vice versa*. His report tabulated what he described as a 'community of interests' among the directors at the heart of the German economy. Hobson, a labour activist and journalist, drew on his experiences reporting the Boer War in South Africa to add a section on corporate power to the Second Edition of his study of *The Evolution of Modern Capitalism* (Hobson 1906). Taking up popular comment on the 'Randlords', the leading gold and diamond producers of South Africa, he tabulated the director-ships held and their formation into an 'inner ring' of finance. The arguments of Jeidels and Hobson were important influences on Marxist work by Rudolf Hilferding (1910) and Vladimir Lenin (1917), who documented the emergence of a dominant group of 'finance capitalists' who had become the leading elements in the various financial groups that pursued strategies of imperial expansion across the globe.

Hobson, however, had gone beyond numerical tabulation and had produced a diagrammatic representation of the inner ring. Most probably inspired by radical metaphors of the 'webs' of influence and the 'tentacles' of large business groups, Hobson drew a schematic and simplified diagram in which circles representing financial groups were connected through a mesh of criss-crossing lines, to numerous industrial ventures. Hobson's suggestive innovation was taken up by a US congres-sional subcommittee enquiry into the monopolistic power of the so-called Money Trust (US Congress 1913). The report not only tabulated the distribution of directorships but also produced large charts in which the connections among the large compa-nies and corporate groups were laid out as maps of corporate power.

The congressional report introduced, or at least popularised, the term 'interlocking' directorships. When one individual holds a board-level position in two companies, the two boards, or directorates, are connected. This 'interlock' is a social rela-tion between the two companies and was seen as a channel of communication and potential influence between business entities that the law and economic theory regard as separate sovereign bodies. Thus, numerical tabulations of directorships can be seen as reports of the quantitative significance of this structure of power. This assumption became the basis on which many later investigations by academics, governmental bodies, and others aimed to investigate the monopolistic powers of top bankers and industrialists regarded as the elite of financial controllers.

A key theme in this research was the attempt to discover and document the particular financial groups that lay at the heart of modern economies. Variously described as 'interest groups' or 'empires' of finance, these groups were not, however, always defined in clear or strict sociometric terms as cliques or components. They were seen as groups of companies subject to common control, but no precise measure of control and hence of the boundaries of this control were specified. The resulting indeterminacy is apparent in the fact that studies of the same economy at similar times have reported different numbers of financial groups. Thus, Marxist economist Paul Sweezy (1939) undertook an investigation for the National Resources Committee of the US Congress in which he documented eight such groups associated with various of the leading investment banks. By the 1950s and 1960s, estimates of group structure varied widely: Perlo reported eight groups but Dooley (1969) reported 15 and Menshikov (1969) reported 22.

The first study of interlocks to introduce proper techniques of social network analysis was that of Warner and Unwalla (1967). Drawing on ideas that had been developing since Warner had himself introduced the idea of the 'clique', Warner and Unwalla described the structure of the US economy as organised around a 'hub' of finance companies with 'spokes' that radiate out into the wider economy. While this remained a metaphorical description, they did report its structure through tabulations of the 'direction' that could be attached to an interlock. When a director holds a full-time executive position within a company, which can thus be regarded as his or her principal business interest, the interlocks created can be seen as an outgoing relation from the base company. From the standpoint of other companies it is an incoming relation from the base company. These two types of interlock, Warner and Unwalla argued, can have a different significance for the companies involved. Later research has distinguished these 'primary interlocks' from the 'induced interlocks' that result among the companies on which the executive sits as a non-executive director and the 'secondary interlocks' that are created by directors who are completely without executive positions (Stokman et al. 1985).

Over the following years, a number of studies have used more rigorous sociometric ideas. Levine (1972) and Bearden et al. (1975) used the new ideas being produced by Harrison White and his colleagues and students to measure centrality in corporate networks and the function of the cliques and clusters formed around central companies. At the same time, Mokken and Stokman oversaw an investigation of the Dutch economy (Helmers and others 1975) and put together a large international research group to study interlock patterns in ten countries (Stokman et al. 1985). Bearden and his associates used a measure of centrality based on the idea of closeness and that took account of direction. They documented the existence of an extensive national network of predominantly 'weak' ties (secondary and induced interlocks) within which could be found more intensely-linked clusters based on the 'strong' ties (primary interlocks) created by executives. The clusters were organised around focal banks and these bank-centred groups were loosely integrated into an extensive national network.

The group led by Mokken and Stokman used the concept of the component to identify any clearly bounded corporate groups that there may be in the Dutch economy. An analysis of undirected interlocks found a single large component containing 84 companies. A breakdown into subgroups on the basis of their densities disclosed a smaller 'core' group and a surrounding periphery. While the core of 17 central companies had a density of 0.76, the density of the whole network was just 0.19. Thus, they argued, the 17 central companies formed a densely connected group of financial companies with influence over the other 67 companies in the large component.

Scott and Griff (1984) used component analysis to show that the largest 250 companies in Britain in 1976 were formed into one large component of 185 and just two smaller components. An analysis based on the value of the lines—the number of directors in common between two companies—showed the existence of many more components, the largest containing just 17 companies. A major part of their analysis, however, concerns cliques identifiable in the network of interlocks carried by executives. The 156 companies in the large component of the network of such primary interlocks contained eight 2-cliques that varied in size from 10 to 15. The central points within each clique were largely taken by banks or insurance companies.

The British network of 1976, therefore, comprised a structure of overlapping bank-centred spheres of influence. It was within and through these spheres that the bank and industry executives who dominated their boards were able to exercise a degree of control and influence over the companies and it was through the overlapping relations of the larger structure of the weak ties that they could ensure a degree of coordination across the economy as a whole.

Levine (1972) recognised the problems involved in drawing sociograms for large networks and so used multidimensional scaling to chart structures of centrality and influence among 70 industrial companies linked to the 14 largest banks of 1966. A three-dimensional representation showed that these interlocks had a regional pattern, that banks were the most central companies, and that the third dimension sharply separated the banks from the industrials. Levine explored this third dimension further using cartographic techniques. Banks, he argued, stood at the centres of clusters of influence and these clusters could be mapped as discrete spaces on the surface of a sphere.

This remarkable burst of research between 1972 and 1985 contained all the key themes to emerge in the social network analysis of corporate interlocks. Subsequent studies have applied similar ideas to different economies, or have taken longitudinal approaches to changes in corporate interlocks over time. One area of strong development, however, has been the attention accorded to transnational networks. Meindert Fennema (1982) had undertaken an analysis of international links and had showed the persistence of national and regional—generally language-based—clusterings. The growing globalisation of economic relationships, however, has led many to investigate whether such nation-state-centred structures have disappeared. David Smith and Doug White (Smith and White 1992) pointed the way with a study of networks of international trading patterns that used blockmodelling to document the existence of trading blocks and their relationship to Wallerstein's world-system categories of core, semi-periphery, and periphery. This kind of approach was taken up in interlock studies by Fennema and Carroll (2002) to investigate the formation and structure of a transnational business community of people with attenuated links to particular national economies.

Further reading

Rogers, Everett 1962. *Diffusion of Innovations*, 5th Edition. New York: Free Press, 2003. The definitive overview of diffusion studies and approaches.

Coleman, James S., Katz, E. and Menzel, H. 1966. *Medical Innovation: A Diffusion Study*. New York: Bobbs-Merrill. Remains a classic study in the application of diffusion methods.

White, Howard D. 2011. 'Scientific and scholarly networks. In *The Sage Handbook of Social Network Analysis*, John Scott and Peter J. Carrington, eds. London: Sage Publications. A clear and definitive account of citation and bibliometric methods.

Mullins, Nicholas C. 1973. *Theories and Theory Groups in American Sociology*. New York: Harper and Row. An early example of work on scientific networks that is especially accessible for students of sociology.

Pennings, Johannes 1980. *Interlocking Directorates*. San Francisco: Jossey-Bass. Chapters 1 and 2 provide one of the few general accounts of this methodology for studying corporate power.

Carroll, William K. 2004. *Corporate Power in a Globalizing World. A Study in Elite Social Organization*. Ontario: Oxford University Press. A powerful recent example of work in this area.

Applications of social network analysis in other areas and specialisms include:

Wellman, Barry 1979. 'The community question: the intimate networks of East Yorkers'. *American Journal of Sociology* 84: 1201–31. An important and influential report on community structure and personal networks.

Werbner, Pnina 1990. *The Migration Process: Capital, Gifts and Offerings among British Pakistanis*. Oxford: Berg Publishers. Uses blockmodelling techniques to investigate migration patterns.

Gould, Roger V. 1995. *Insurgent Identities: Class, Community and Protest in Paris from 1848 to the Commune*. Chicago: University of Chicago Press. Uses network techniques to investigate class formation and solidarity.

Bearman, Peter S. 1993. *Relations into Rhetorics: Local Elite Social Structure in Norfolk, England: 1540–1640*. Rutgers: Rutgers University Press. An historical study using legal records to investigate aristocratic class relations.

A range of specialised papers can be found in:

Scott, John and Carrington, Peter, eds 2011. *The Sage Handbook of Social Network Analysis*, London: Sage Publications. Section 2 includes Chapters reviewing work on social support, online communities, policy networks, terrorist networks, criminal networks, cultural networks, and many other topics.

Scott, John ed. 2002 *Social Networks: Critical Concept*, Four Volumes. London: Routledge. A collection of classic sources. Volumes 2 and 3 cover family and community; Volume 3 covers corporate power and economic structure, and Volume 4 covers politics, protest, and policy networks.

5 Criticisms and frequently asked questions

Social network analysis is a collection of concepts, measures, and techniques for relational analysis. It is an approach that is specifically designed to grasp the most important features of social structures and it is unrivalled in this task. It can be used to explore social relations themselves and also the cultural structures of norms and ideas that help to organise those relations in conjunction with material circumstances. The various applications reviewed in Chapter 4 have demonstrated the ways in which relational and cultural structures can be investigated with a few simple network concepts. Theories of social structure inform and sustain the methods of social network analysis.

The social world, however, consists of more than just social structures (Scott 2011a), and social network analysis itself cannot reach beyond the structural concerns for which it was designed. Many of the issues that arise in the study of social action require a totally different set of theoretical ideas: ideas concerning motives, intentions, rationality, emotionality, and subjectivity together with the consequences, intended and unintended, to which different types of action lead. Action theories therefore require different methods and techniques—methods of frame analysis and interpretation, for example—and a crucial question in sociology concerns the complementarity or opposition between theories of structure and action. My own view is that they are not contradictory or alternative to each other but are complementary. Indeed, I have shown in Chapter 2 that dynamic models of network development rest upon a combination of structural ideas and a theory of action and its consequences.

It is equally the case that cultural analysis involves more than just the analysis of cultural structure. The study of culture rests upon ideas of discourse, ideology, representation, and socialisation that are specific to cultural analysis and require specific methods of their own: content analysis, narrative analysis, ideology critique, and so on. These ideas, too, are complementary to the structural ideas behind social network analysis. A number of works in network analysis have now begun to combine these frameworks together (see, for example, Mische 2007).

Thus, social network analysis is closely linked to structural theories and, as such, comprises one element in a more comprehensive framework of sociological analysis. Action theories and cultural theories, with their associated methods, are complementary within this framework. Social network analysis is limited to its structural concerns, but it is an essential complement to other, equally limited, approaches. The use of social network analysis in particular research projects is likely, therefore, to require the use of a variety of other methods of data collection and analysis. Even in its own territory, social network analysis is likely to involve a multi-method research design, and it is rarely the case that even a predominantly structural study will use social network techniques alone. This is equally the case with respect to data collection. The collection of data for social network analysis involves methods of data collection that are not specific to it: most particularly, survey methods, ethnographic methods, and documentary methods. An understanding of social structure in the context of the actions of individuals and groups and the cultural contexts in which they live and construct their actions will involve placing social network analysis alongside the other analytical methods appropriate to these areas. These multiple methods of data collection and analysis—both quantitative and qualitative—must be combined in an appropriately devised research design.

These limitations to social network analysis are fundamental, though they are no different from the limitations that apply to any specialised approach. However, some potentially serious limitations have been suggested by critics of network analysis, and these must be considered and answered.

Criticisms and responses

Network analysis, like all social research methods, has been the subject of much criticism by those whose preferences and intellectual concerns lie in different directions. Indeed, social network analysis has, perhaps, received more than its fair share of criticism, and perhaps some of this criticism has been provoked by the overstatements—or even the naivety—of some of its advocates and users. Much criticism, however, is based upon misunderstanding and misrepresentation. In this section I will address the major criticisms and try to show how much credence should be accorded to them. I will look at six commonly voiced criticisms:

1   Isn't it all frightfully new and exciting?
2   Isn't it all rather trivial?
3   Isn't it all unnecessary?
4   Isn't it just pretty pictures?
5   Isn't it simply too formal?
6   Isn't it very static?

1   *Isn't it all frightfully new and exciting?*

This statement is not so much a criticism as a complete misrepresentation of the history of social network analysis. During the late 1990s, a number of physicists put forward mathematical models of networks that, they held, could be applied widely in social science applications and could fill a huge intellectual gap in sociological understanding. Social scientists, they argued, had simply ignored the fact that people are connected into structures of social relations that can be analysed in terms of their distinctive emergent properties. Thus, this comment was a criticism of the poor intellectual skills of social scientists, who had failed to understand how important were the social networks in which people are involved and had to wait until the physicists came along and showed them how to do relational sociology. This view was enthusiastically taken up by non-social scientists and by journalists and other commentators. Many books and articles appeared and enthused over the 'new science' of social networks. We live in an increasingly 'connected' world, they argued, and so we require these new techniques if we are to study this new phenomenon.

I have shown in Chapter 2 that social network analysis has, in fact, a long history in sociology, anthropology, and social psychology: a history reaching back to the early days of these disciplines. Even if attention is limited to formal and systematic mathematical approaches, this history stretches back for over half a century. So what, exactly, is going on? Why have physicists and recent commentators not been aware of this history?

It has to be recognised that, to a degree, social network analysts have themselves been culpable. Rather than actively proselytising beyond their disciplinary boundaries, they have simply got on with the job and have carried out their specialised studies. Unless people have read the sociological literature they will not have been aware of the work in social network analysis. This is why those who advocate this 'new' method are so completely wrong. In claiming the critical need for their own approach to sociological questions, they forgot to check whether sociologists had got there first: they simply did not bother to look at any sociology (or, for that matter, any anthropology or social psychology) before decrying the absence of relational concerns in those disciplines (Scott 2011b).

Social network analysis, as practiced by social scientists, may not be new but it is certainly exciting. The critics of social science have got it right on this point at least. I hope that I have shown in Chapter 4 and elsewhere that social network analysis provides powerful and exciting insights into crucially important questions and that the techniques outlined in this book can help us to explore these.

2 *Isn't it all rather trivial?*

Those who point to the triviality of social network analysis do recognise that this particular specialism exists, but they fail to recognise what it is actually about. The claim is often made these days that sociologists who study social networks ought really to be studying something more important. The study of social networks is seen as concerned with the 'social networking' promoted by management consultants and the use of internet-based 'social network' sites such as Facebook, Twitter, My Space, and LinkedIn. This, many people assume, is what social network analysis is all about.

The first point to make is that these phenomena are, in fact, rather important social phenomena. An increasing amount of communication and interaction is now internet-based and people engage with each other through e-mail, live messaging, and dedicated websites to an ever greater extent. The cyber world is an increasingly important part of all our social worlds. However, social network analysis does not only concern itself with these web-mediated forms of interaction. It is concerned with the whole range of face-to-face and spatially distanciated social relations that have always been the principal objects of sociological analysis.

Some critics, even within the discipline, have recognised this point but persist with their criticism of the triviality—or perhaps marginality—of social network analysis. This approach, they argue, is concerned only with the interpersonal relations of everyday life and cannot be used to investigate more important matters of economic and political structure or the many macro-social features of human life. This criticism is misguided on two grounds. First, the interpersonal and the everyday are every bit as important as the economic and the political. There are no grounds for asserting the triviality or importance of one domain of enquiry over another. Second, social network analysis *is* able to address economic, political, and macro-social issues. I have illustrated this in Chapter 4, where I showed the long history of research into economic structures of relations that have investigated national economic structures and the structures of global economic systems.

Social network analysis, far from being trivial or concerned with marginal issues, has addressed central social issues across the whole spectrum of the discipline. It is an approach of major significance.

3 Isn't it all unnecessary?

This criticism may not see social network analysis as limited to triviality, but it does hold that the findings of social network analysis are lacking in significance. This is the oft-cited 'so what?' criticism of social network analysis. Such critics note the immense time and effort spent on documenting the number and type of ties that link people together into more or less dense chains of connection but go on to ask that the analyst show that these make some difference to how people act or to the outcomes of their actions. Critics claim that everybody knows that such links exist and that anyone, with the appropriate technical skills, can map them out, but unless it can be shown that people take some account of them or that things are different because of them, then the research findings are merely documents of the obvious and the irrelevant. The most radical of these critics go on to assert that even if the researcher did try to assess the importance of network connections, he or she would inevitably find that they have no importance. All this research is, therefore, completely unnecessary.

It has to be said that much social network analysis has, in fact, remained at the purely descriptive level and has not gone on to assess the significance of the connections for the individuals involved. Some early computer-based research did report measures simply because the available software made them easy to compute: 'if it can be measured then it must be significant' was their assumption. This kind of naïve empiricism also marked early uses of SPSS for survey analysis, where the option 'Statistics all' spewed out an array of statistics that were assumed to be important simply because they were a part of the package. However, this assumption is far from typical. I have argued in Chapter 3 that it is essential that the structural analyst know and understand the concepts that are being used and that he or she can justify them as valid and appropriate. When there is a prima facie reason to expect the social relations to have an effect, then a descriptive mapping plays an essential part in the research process. This is typically the case when a project is firmly grounded in an on-going tradition of research in which this significance has been explored or inferred. I have shown in Chapter 3 that there have been good technical reasons why conventional statistical significance tests cannot be used in social network analysis and that it is only now that appropriate methods of statistical analysis have become available.

The 'so what?' criticism has always carried less weight than its users believe. It is a criticism that could be raised against *any* approach to sociology where there is an absence of accepted theoretical justification or established empirical grounding. Using survey analysis to document the pattern of attitudes held among the members of a group, for example, could be subjected to the same criticism unless the researcher produced a theoretical rationale for the significance of the distribution of attitudes or rehearsed the results of empirical studies. Much survey research is just as descriptive as much social network research, and the fact that the 'so what?' question is raised against one rather than the other smacks more of prejudice than of reasoned argument. Happily, such criticisms are becoming less frequent as social network analysis becomes more established and its research applications can allude to a larger theoretical and empirical framework to legitimate its use.

4 Isn't it just pretty pictures?

This is really a variant of the 'so what?' criticism and so can be dealt with briefly. The criticism is particularly applied to studies that concentrate on the display of sociograms rather than the calculation of specific measures. The argument is that drawing a sociogram, however colourful and striking, must still be shown to be a 'real' social factor with distinct causal effects on actions and their outcomes. While the validity of this argument can be recognised, exactly the same considerations are relevant as have been discussed in relation to the larger 'so what?' criticism.

5 Isn't it simply too formal?

This criticism implies a dualism between 'structure' and 'action', arguing that the formal clarity of network structure ignores the meanings and definitions through which people construct their social relations. Sociological explanations, they argue, must take account of individual definitions of the situation and must recognise that the particular formal connections discovered by an outside observer are important factors in sociological analysis only if and in so far as they are taken account of by individuals. It is the individuals who interpret social relations that give them their significance. The further conclusion is drawn that particular connections—a directorship, a citation, a friendship—will mean different things to different people and so it is meaningless to treat them all as equivalent and to count them up or use them in formal methodologies.

This is an important criticism if not taken to its extreme. Social relations do vary in their significance for individual actors and it is not at all straightforward to count numbers of friends or to rate one friendship as twice or three times as important as another. However, the difficulty in doing this does not warrant the conclusion that it is impossible. It is always necessary for social researchers to make an informed, expert judgement about the meaning and significance of social relations to individuals, but this must be done on the basis of evidence that warrants the judgement as plausible. Counting, ranking, and valuing relationships for use in social network analysis do not involve making an essential and absolute statement about what the relationship 'really' means to individuals. Use of these procedures is an attempt to find a plausible and defensible way of transcending individual subjectivity and drawing some general conclusions. It is simply one particular way of undertaking a relational, structural analysis and only if the very idea of structural analysis is rejected can the criticism be upheld in full. I have tried to argue above that it cannot be rejected and that structural analysis has a part to play alongside other approaches to sociology.

6 Isn't it very static?

This final criticism has been thoroughly covered already. Critics argue, however, that social network analysis has been static and descriptive because this is all it ever can be. Social network analysis, they argue, simply charts relationships and structures as they exist at a particular time. Even if the critics do not claim that this work is unnecessary, they do claim that it is fundamentally limited and can tell only a small part of the whole story. Social relations are changing all the time and a snapshot picture taken at a particular point might be an extremely poor representation of the social structure at a later time.

This is an important criticism, though it involves a considerable overstatement. It is true that a single cross-section, or even a series of them, is a poor representation of a continually changing social process. It is similarly the case that screen shots give a poor impression of a movie. However, when used with care, descriptive studies can serve as the first step towards more comprehensive accounts. They are the starting point—not the end point—of on-going research. As I showed in Chapter 3, methods better able to grasp dynamic processes and that allow proper longitudinal research to be undertaken are now becoming available and are being more widely used. We all have to walk before we can run, and the new mathematical concepts and software programs allow the social network analyst to take this further step.

Frequently asked questions

In the first part of this chapter I have looked at some of the principal questions raised by critics of social network analysis, and I have tried to provide some responses to these. In this part of the chapter I turn to the practical questions raised by those who think they might find social network analysis useful but are concerned about their own abilities to use or to understand the techniques required. In most cases, the answers should be apparent from the earlier, detailed discussions, but I have tried to highlight the key issues here. Seven questions recur in practical discussions of how to do a social network study:

1   How can I decide who to include as members of my network?
2   When do I stop tracing connections among the members of my group?
3   How can I decide the relative importance of different kinds of network linkage?
4   How can I determine the strength of intensity of a social relation?
5   Networks include positive as well as negative relations: does this pose problems for social network analysis?

6   Do I need to know a lot of mathematics to use social network analysis?

7   What are the ethics of social network analysis; isn't it just a form of snooping and spying?

1   *How can I decide who to include as members of my network?*

This is the issue of the so-called 'boundary problem' in social network analysis. In some cases, the boundaries of a network will be clear and straightforward: the members of a school class or year group, the members of an organisation, and so on. However, groups that may appear to be clearly bounded may actually be indeterminate. It might at first seem obvious who to include as members of a family, for example, but does the 'family' include aunts, uncles, and cousins, what degrees of cousinhood are relevant, and what are the implications of divorce, remarriage, or cohabitation? Can the same definition be used in all cases: does each potential member of the network mean the same thing by 'family'? Boundaries must usually be determined by the informed expert judgement of the researcher and can rarely be decided on the basis of network measures themselves. A sociologist of the family, for example, must decide what, in the light of existing knowledge, makes sense as a definition of the family and so how it is to be bounded. Similarly, an economic sociologist must decide, on the basis of prior research, whether a network of 'top' companies should include 100, 200, or 300 companies. There are, in fact, no easy answers to these questions, but that is true of any sociological question worth asking.

2 When do I stop tracing connections among the members of my group?

It is very easy to get carried away and to record long chains of connection: to note down friends of the friends of a worker who are committee members of political parties in which other members are friends of the friends of an employer. This does not necessarily mean that the worker and his or her employer have any significant social relationship beyond the employment relationship itself. As with the boundary question, the investigator must decide on the basis of sociological evidence and conceptualisation when to cut-off the search for relationships. Equally, the investigator him or herself must decide whether relations involving, say, line distances of five, six, or more constitute real social relationships or can be regarded as having a sociological significance. This decision is likely to vary from one type of relationship to another.

3 How can I decide the relative importance of different kinds of network linkage?

This is not something that social network analysis itself can resolve for you. Most relationships are complex and involve many different emotions, purposes, and interests: social network analysts describe them as 'multiplex'. Someone may, for example, be simultaneously a friend, workmate, and political collaborator of another, and any separation of 'friendship', 'work relation', and 'political affiliation' is likely to be arbitrary. Nevertheless, this is what sociologists must do in constructing ideal types of relations from concrete patterns of connection. This analytical approach to social relations is a prelude to deciding which is to be seen as the most important for the practical purpose at hand. When a number of potentially important relations have been identified, however, social network analysis does provide a way of calculating which of these seems to have the greatest salience or significance for the particular question being investigated: this is simply the standard form of causal analysis in social science.

4 How can I determine the strength of intensity of a social relation?

At the risk of repetition, this depends on your expert sociological judgement. The strength of a relationship in social network analysis is simply the number that is attached to the line, and this number is something that has to be decided during the research process. The researcher must use some kind of sociologically grounded criterion of scaling in order to assign numerical values to a line. This is relatively straightforward when deciding on the absence or presence of a relation and so assigning a value of 0 or 1, but even here it may not always be obvious when a relationship has ceased to exist or come into being. It is far more difficult to assign a value of 2 to one line and 4 to another, and it may be highly problematic to conclude that the latter is twice as strong as the former. In social network analysis this is technically described as the problem of linearity in ratio scales. All that can be said is that, as in all sociological analyses worth undertaking, a plausible and justifiable estimate of strength must be made and that this tentative and arbitrary estimation must be remembered when it comes to analysing your results. Don't forget that *you* assigned the numbers in the first place and so the results will reflect the plausibility of that initial judgement.

5 Networks include positive as well as negative relations: does this pose problems for social network analysis?

Yes, it does, but only because it poses problems for the people involved! Negative relations of dislike, withdrawal, exclusion, or conflict may cause discomfort for the people involved, but for the sociologist they pose no additional questions. A + or − sign can be assigned to indicate their character and they can then be treated in exactly the same way as any other relationship. A negative relationship can be assigned a numerical value in the same way as a positive one and, of course, all the same limitations will apply.

6 Do I need to know a lot of mathematics to use social network analysis?

The simple answer is 'no'. The more complex answer is 'maybe'. The basic concepts and measures used in social network analysis can all be generated very rapidly by the standard, and easy to use, software packages described in the following chapter. To do this requires absolutely no mathematical expertise and depends simply on your skills with a keyboard and mouse to negotiate the menu structure of the software. However, you do need to have some understanding of what the various procedures are trying to do and whether it makes sense to use them for your data. This is the kind of understanding that I have tried to provide in Chapter 3 and, in more detail, in my handbook of social network analysis (Scott 2012). In order to follow the discussions in some of the more advanced texts, however, you will need to have some familiarity with mathematical notation and procedures, though not generally of a very high level. More important is the willingness to grapple with the numbers and symbols and to expect some difficulty in comprehension. As with any difficult enterprise in social science, the benefits outweigh the heartaches.

7 What are the ethics of social network analysis; isn't it just a form of snooping and spying?

All sociology is a form of snooping: that's what makes it such fun! Studying networks is no more unethical that studying any other aspect of a person's life. It is important, of course, to observe the normal considerations of confidentiality and anonymity where these are requested and are appropriate, but the application and use of social network analysis raises no additional problems to those found with any other social research method. There have been concerns over the use of social network analysis by the police and the security services to investigate criminal and terrorist networks and networks of political activists. There are very genuine issues about whether academic social scientists should cooperate in such research, but the validity of undertaking this research is not a question of professional ethics but is a much larger political question about the legitimate role and scope of state activity. Social network analysis is not 'value free', but neither is it an especially unethical form of social science.

Further reading

Scott, John and Carrington, Peter 2011. *The Sage Handbook of Social Network Analysis*. London: Sage Publications. Section 1 includes reviews of developments in social network analysis in various disciplines and considers the theoretical issues raised in these. The Chapters by John Scott and by Bettina Holstein are especially relevant to the issues discussed here.

Cresswell, John W. and Plano Clark, V. L. 2007. *Designing and conducting mixed methods research*. Thousand Oaks, CA: Sage Publications. A general souerce that does not discuss social network analysis but gives a clear statement and rationale for combined or multiple methods.

6 Software for social network analysis

As I outlined in Chapter 1, the time was that many of the processes involved in social network analysis had to be undertaken manually. Even when computers came into wide use, the possibilities for rapid data analysis were limited by the need to refine, or even to provide from scratch, software programs that would automate some of the basic tasks. All this has changed. A number of software programs are now both easily and cheaply available, and the newcomer to social network analysis can rapidly begin to produce sophisticated analyses of her or his data. This situation has its dangers, of course. The temptation to generate output is such that a researcher may produce that output first and only then consider whether it is useful or, indeed, valid. However, having got this far in this book, I hope that my readers will be very aware of this problem and will not fall into that trap.

In this chapter I want to provide a general guide to the use of some of the most important packages available. In order to use these effectively you may want to work through some of the more technical readings given in Chapter 3, but this guide should provide you with enough information to allow you to begin producing some simple, but quite powerful, measures of network structure.

Two programs dominate the field: UCINET and PAJEK. UCINET is a commercial programme distributed by Analytical Technologies (http://www.analytictech.com/). PAJEK is a freely distributed programme available from a WIKI site (http://pajek.imfm.si/doku.php?id=pajek). A word of warning: this webpage includes a large photograph of a spider and the squeamish may prefer to go directly to (http://pajek.imfm.si/doku.php?id=download)! Each program has its particular advantages and limitations, and a choice may be a matter of personal preference. This choice may be quite easy to make as UCINET includes PAJEK as an add-in for its own program code. In addition to these general programs there is a widely used statistical program, R, that includes a specialist add-on for the statistical analysis of social network data. This program is more complex to use, but is extremely powerful and makes it possible to transfer data to other statistical and graphical routines. These are the three principal programs on which I will concentrate, but I will also make some brief reference to a number of specialist visualisation programs that are associated with them and, in some cases, distributed with them as add-ons.

UCINET: *The pioneer program*

UCINET was developed at the Irvine campus of the University of California (UC, Irvine—hence the acronym). It was designed and

produced by some of the leading social network researchers—
most notably, Lin Freeman, Steve Borgatti, and Martin Everett—
as a way of helping others to undertake the kinds of analyses that
they themselves were using in their empirical studies. It is now
available in Version 6 and is established as a tried and tested, and
very stable, platform for social network analysis.

UCINET appears on screen with a very simple menu structure,
from which data entry and information windows appear. Seven
top-level menu headings define the structure of the program:

- FILE
- DATA
- TRANSFORM
- TOOLS
- NETWORK
- VISUALIZE
- OPTIONS

As might be expected, the FILE menu provides access to the basic
file management tasks and access to its current add-ins. The core
of the program, however, is to be found under the DATA menu,
together with the TRANSFORM menu. DATA is the gateway to
data entry and the import and export functions. From here it is
possible to compile a data file in native UCINET format—typically simply the network as a linked list of data points—or to
import the raw data from text files and spread sheets. The DATA
menu also provides the routines needed to refine and prepare
data sets, using extraction and deletion procedures to determine
the inclusion or exclusion of particular points and subgroups.
Finally, the DATA menu allows for the sorting, permutation, and

transposing of the basic data and for converting it into different formats. For example, the conversion of 2-mode into 1-mode data is achieved in this way. TRANSFORM provides further options for dichotomising or slicing a network. All these tasks are handled very intuitively, with the option given at each stage to save any newly generated files. There is also a useful provision of error messages that can be supplemented by the comprehensive 'Help' screens.

The TOOLS menu in UCINET leads to procedures for undertaking some basic, auxiliary tasks. This is the way in which it is possible to use cluster analysis—and to construct dendrograms from clustered data—and to undertake metric and non-metric multidimensional scaling, factor analysis, and correspondence analysis. The key network concepts and measures are to be found, unsurprisingly, under the NETWORK menu. Here are to be found measures of distance, density, homophily, and centrality, as well as methods for identifying components, cliques, structurally equivalent blocks, and other subgroups. It is also through the NETWORK menu that a number of egocentric measures can be produced, including analyses of betweenness and brokerage.

Particularly useful features of UCINET are the routines found under its VISUALIZE menu. It is here that the NETDRAW network-drawing package, the MAGE modelling program, and the drawing facilities provided in PAJEK can be accessed. These are all discussed below.

PAJEK

PAJEK—Slovenian for 'spider'—was developed at the University of Ljubljana by Vladimir Batagelj and his colleagues. It had its origins as a specialist program for handling very large data sets and includes a number of advanced measures. The program has a more extensive menu structure than UCINET and does not cover quite the same wide range of measures, but a number of key measures are provided in addition to its ability to analyse large data sets very rapidly. A manual for the program has been published as an accessible guide to social network analysis (De Nooy *et al.* 2005).

The basic elements in the program are to be found under the FILE and NET menus. Here can be found the routines for inputting and editing network data and for exporting data in various formats, such as that of UCINET. The NET menu provides various routines for transforming networks, much as are provided in UCINET's DATA and TRANSFORM menus, though sorting is accessed under the OPERATIONS menu. NET is also the means through which components can be identified, while the OPERATIONS menu allows the undertaking of blockmodelling.

The heart of the PAJEK program for many of its users is its DRAW menu, which leads to a screen from which sub-menus allow the drawing and displaying of networks and their subgroups. Simple circle diagrams can be drawn, but the most interesting option is, perhaps, the ability to generate two-dimensional and three-dimensional visualisations based on forms of multidimensional scaling. Visual representations can be produced easily, and three-dimensional representations can be rotated in various ways to display and inspect a network. Simple but powerful techniques are available to include or exclude labels for data points and to indicate the value or intensity of a line. The representations produced can be exported in various graphics formats for printing or for display independently of the PAJEK program.

R and other programs

R (available at http://www.r-project.org/) is a program produced as part of a general project for statistical computing. It comprises a basic framework that serves as a platform for a number of supplied modules and add-ons that all operate within its basic environment. The two most important add-ons for social network analysis are STATNET and SIENA. STATNET covers the important techniques for hypothesis testing associated with ERGM methods. SIENA was originally developed by Tom Snijders as part of his StOCNET program, now supplanted by R. SIENA is especially geared to the statistical analysis of longitudinal and cross-sectional data, so allowing the assessment of the significance of change over time.

Other, free-standing, programs that readers may wish to investigate are NETDRAW, MAGE, and SONIA. NETDRAW, also provided as a module within UCINET, is a powerful program for drawing and editing basic network sociograms. It interfaces rapidly with UCINET and works rapidly on its files. MAGE was devised by chemists as a way of using stick and ball methods to represent chemical bonding formulae (see http://kinemage.

biochem.duke.edu/kinemage/magepage.php). Because of its data structure it is adapted easily for use in social network analysis and provides both two-dimensional and three-dimensional representations of data generated from UCINET or PAJEK and allows the 'sticks' and 'balls' of a network (the lines and points) to be coloured and labelled in various ways. SONIA, devised by Snijders and supported by Dan McFarland and Skye Bender de Moll, is a visualisation package for longitudinal data (see http://www.stanford.edu/group/sonia/). Unlike the programs discussed so far, SONIA works under JAVA and requires the installation of at least the basic JAVA package. The environment gives the program the ability to produce striking and easily transportable visual representations of social network data as moving images.

As all the best marketing presentations say: other network programs are available. A guide to these can be found in Huisman and van Duijn (2011). The programs discussed in this chapter, however, are the most easily accessible and useable programs for the beginner and for more advanced users. If I can be permitted a recommendation, I will suggest using UCINET, which gives direct and integrated access to PAJEK, NETDRAW, and MAGE. Used as an adjunct to your reading of more advanced texts on social network analysis, the program and its add-ons will allow you to do almost anything you can imagine—and many things that you are unlikely to have imagined. As your knowledge improves, you will find that you need to use R and SONIA, and you should, by then, have the technical ability to handle them and to use them sensibly.

Bibliography

Alba, Richard D. and Kadushin, Charles 1976. 'The intersection of social circles: a new measure of social proximity in networks'. *Sociological Methods and Research* 5.

Barabási, Albert-László 2002. *Linked: The New Science of Networks*. Cambridge, Mass.: Perseus.

Barnes, John A. 1954. 'Class and committee in a Norwegian island parish'. *Human Relations* 7.

Bearden, James and others 1975. 'The nature and extent of bank centrality in corporate networks' in Scott, J. (ed.) *Social Networks, Volume 3*. London: Sage, 2002.

Bogardus, Emory S. 1925. 'Measuring social distance'. *Journal of Applied Sociology* 9.

Bogardus, Emory S. 1959. *Social Distance*. Los Angeles: Antioch Press.

Boorman, Scott A. and White, Harrison C. 1976. 'Social structure from multiple networks: II'. *American Journal of Sociology* 81.

Bott, Elizabeth 1957. *Family and Social Network*. London: Tavistock Publications.

Bott, Helen 1928. 'Observation of play activities in a nursery school'. *Genetic Psychology Monographs* 4: 44–8.

Bourdieu, Pierre 1979. *Distinction: A Social Critique of the Judgment of Taste*. London: Routledge, 1984.

Burt, Ronald S. 1987. 'Social contagion and innovation: cohesion versus structural equivalence'. *American Journal of Sociology* 92, 6: 1287–1335.

Burt, Ronald S. 1992. *Structural Holes*. New York: Cambridge University Press.

Burt, Ronald S. 2005. *Brokerage and Closure: An Introduction to Social Capital*. New York: Oxford University Press.

Cartwright, D. and Zander, A. (eds.) 1953. *Group Dynamics*. London: Tavistock.

Coleman, James S., Katz, E. and Menzel, H. 1966. *Medical Innovation: A Diffusion Study*. New York: Bobbs-Merrill.

Collins, Randall 2000. *The Sociology of Philosophers*. Cambridge, Mass.: Harvard University Press.

Coxon, Anthony P. M. 1982. *The Users' Guide to Multidimensional Scaling*. London: Heinemann.

Crane, Diana 1972. *Invisible Colleges. The Diffusion of Knowledge in Scientific Communities*. Chicago: University of Chicago Press.

Davis, Allisson B., Gardner, B. B. and Gardner, M. R. 1941. *Deep South*. Chicago: University of Chicago Press.

Davis, James A 1963. 'Structural balance, mechanical solidarity and interpersonal relations'. *American Journal of Sociology* 68: 444–462.

De Nooy, Wouter, Mrvar, Andrej and Batagelj, Vladimir 2005. *Exploratory Social Network Analysis with Pajek*. New York: Cambridge University Press.

Degenne, Alain and Forsé , Michel 1994. *Introducing Social Networks*. English translation, Beverley Hills: Sage Publications, 1999.

Dooley, Peter C. 1969. 'The Interlocking Directorate' in Scott, J. (ed.) *The Sociology of Elites, Volume 3*. Aldershot: Edward Elgar Publishing, 1990.

Everitt, Brian 1974. *Cluster Analysis*. London: Heinemann.

Farrell, Michael P. 2001. *Collaborative Circles. Friendship Dynamics and Creative Work*. Chicago: University of Chicago Press.

Fennema, Meindert 1982. *International Networks of Banks and Industry*. Hague: Martinus Nijhof.

Fennema, Meindert and Carroll, William K. 2002. 'Is there a transnational business community'. *International Sociology* 17, 3: 393–419.

Festinger, Leon 1957. *A Theory of Cognitive Dissonance*. Stanford: Stanford University Press.

Festinger, Leon, Riecken, H. W. and Schachter, S. 1956. *When Prophecy Fails*. New York: Harper and Row.

Fischer, Claude S. 1977. *Networks and Places: Social Relations in the Urban Setting*. New York: Free Press.

Fischer, Claude S. 1982. *To Dwell Among Friends: Personal Networks in Town and City*. Chicago: University of Chicago Press.

French, John R. P. and Raven, Bertram 1959. 'The bases of social power' in Cartwright, D. (ed.) *Studies in Social Power*. Ann Arbor: University of Michigan Press, 1959.

Gould, Roger V. 1993. 'Collective action and network structure'. *American Sociological Review* 58: 182–96.

Gould, Roger V. 1995. *Insurgent Identities. Class, Community, and Protest in Paris from 1848 to the Commune*. Chicago: Chicago University Press.

Granovetter, Mark 1973. 'The strength of weak ties'. *American Journal of Sociology* 78, 6: 1360–1380.

Granovetter, Mark 1974. *Getting A Job*. Cambridge, Mass.: Harvard University Press.

Hall, G. Stanley 1904. *Adolescence. Its Psychology and Its Relation to Psychology, Anthropology, Sociology, Sex, Crime, Religion. Two Volumes*. New York: D. Appleton.

Harary, F. and Norman, R. Z. 1953. *Graph Theory as a Mathematical Model in Social Science*. Ann Arbor: Institute for Social Research.

Helmers, H. M. and others 1975. *Graven Naar Macht*. Amsterdam: Van Gennep.

Hilferding, Rudolf 1910. *Finance Capital*. London: Routledge and Kegan Paul, 1981.

Hobson, John Atkinson 1906. *The Evolution of Modern Capitalism, Revised Edition*. London: George Allen and Unwin.

Homans, George 1950. *The Human Group*. London: Routledge and Kegan Paul, 1951.

Hope, Keith (ed.). 1972. *The Analysis of Social Mobility. Methods and Approaches*. Oxford: Clarendon Press.

Huisman, Mark and van Duijn, Marijtje A. J. 2011. 'A Reader's Guide to SNA Software' in Scott, J. and Carrington, P.C. (eds.) *The Sage Handbook of Social Network Analysis*. London: Sage, 2011.

Jeidels, Otto 1905. *Das Verhältnis der deutschen Grossbanken zur Industrie mit besonderer Berücksichtigung der Eisenindustrie*. Leipzig: Duncker & Humblot.

Jennings, Helen Hall 1948. *Sociometry in Group Relations*. Washington, DC: American Council on Education.

Köhler, Wolfgang 1917. *The Mentality of Apes*. London: Routledge and Kegan Paul, 1924.

Kruskal, Joseph B and Wish, Myron 1978. *Multidimensional Scaling*. Beverly Hills, CA: Sage.

Kuhn, Thomas S. 1962. *The Structure of Scientific Revolutions (Second Edition, 1970)*. Chicago: University of Chicago Press.

Laumann, E. O and Pappi, F. U. 1976. *Networks of Collective Action: A Perspective on Community Influence Systems*. New York: Academic Press.

Laumann, Edward O 1973. *Bonds of Pluralism*. New York: John Wiley.

Laumann, Edward O. 1966. *Prestige and Association in an Urban Community*. Indianapolis: Bobbs-Merrill.

Lenin, Vladimir Ilyich 1917. *Imperialism: The Highest Stage of Capitalism*. Moscow: Progress Publishers, 1966.

Levine, Joel H. 1972. 'The sphere of influence'. *American Sociological Review* 37.

Levine, Joel H. 1984. *Levine's Atlas of Corporate Interlocks*. Hanover, NH: Worldnet.

Lorrain, F. and White, Harrison C. 1971. 'Structural equivalence of individuals in social networks'. *Journal of Mathematical Sociology* 1.

Lundberg, George 1936. 'The sociography of some community relations'. *American Sociological Review* 1, 5.

Lundberg, George and Steele, Mary 1938. 'Social attraction-patterns in a village'. *Sociometry.* 1: 375–419.

Marwell, Gerald and Oliver, Pamela 1993. *The Critical Mass in Collective Action.* Cambridge: Cambridge University Press.

Menshikov, Sergei 1969. *Millionaires and Managers.* Moscow: Progress Publishers.

Milgram, Stanley 1967. 'The small world problem'. *Psychology Today* 2: 60–7.

Mintz, Beth and Schwartz, Michael 1985. *The Power Structure of American Business.* Chicago: Chicago University Press.

Mische, Ann 2007. *Partisan Publics: Communication and Contention across Brazilian Youth Activist Networks.* Princeton, NJ: Princeton University Press.

Mitchell, J. Clyde (ed.). 1969. *Social Networks in Urban Situations.* Manchester: Manchester University Press.

Mizruchi, Mark S. 1982. *The American Corporate Network, 1900 – 1974.* London: Sage.

Moody, James and Light, Ryan 2006. 'A view from above: The evolving sociological landscape'. *American Sociologist* Summer: 67–85.

Moreno, Jacob L. 1934. *Who Shall Survive?* New York: Beacon Press.

Mullins, Nicholas C. 1973. *Theories and Theory Groups in American Sociology.* New York: Harper and Row.

Nadel, Siegfried Frederick 1957. *The Theory of Social Structure.* Glencoe: Free Press.

Oliver, Pamela, Marwell, Gerald and Prahl, Ralph 1988a. 'Social networks and collective action: a theory of critical mass, III'. *American Journal of Sociology* 94: 502–34.

Oliver, Pamela, Marwell, Gerald and Teixeira, Ruy 1985. 'A theory of the critical mass, I'. *American Journal of Sociology* 91: 522–56.

Oliver, Pamela, Marwell, Gerald and Teixeira, Ruy 1988b. 'The paradox of group size in collective action: a theory of the critical mass, II'. *American Sociological review* 53: 1–8.

Oliver, Pamela and Myers, Daniel J. 2003. 'Networks, Diffusion, and Cycles of Collective Action' in Diani, M. and McAdam, D. (eds.) *Social Movements and Networks: Relational Approaches to Collective Action*. Oxford: Oxford University Press, 2003.

Parsons, Talcott 1937. *The Structure of Social Action*. New York: McGraw-Hill.

Pattison, Philippa 1993. *Algebraic Models for Social Networks*. Cambridge: Cambridge University Press.

Prell, Christina 2012. *Social Network Analysis: History, Theory and Methodology*. London: Sage.

Price, Derek de Solla 1963. *Little Science, Big Science*. New York: Columbia University Press.

Radcliffe-Brown, Alfred Reginald 1940. 'On social structure' in Radcliffe-Brown, A.R. (ed.) *Structure and Function in Primitive Society*. London: Cohen and West, 1952.

Roethlisberger, F. J. and Dickson, William J. 1939. *Management and the Worker*. Cambridge, MA: Harvard University Press.

Rogers, Everett 1962. *Diffusion of Innovations, 5th Edition*. New York: Free Press, 2003.

Rouanet, Henri and Le Roux, Brigitte 2009. *Multiple Correspondence Analysis* London: Sage.

Ryan, Bryce and Gross, Neil C. 1943. 'The diffusion of hybrid seed corn in two Iowa communities'. *Rural Sociology* 8: 15–24.

Scott, John 2011a. *Conceptualising the Social World. Principles of Socilogical Analysis.* Cambridge: Cambridge University Press.

Scott, John 2011b. 'The new social physics' in Scott, J. and Carrington, P.J. (eds.) *The Sage Handbook of Social Network Analysis.* London: Sage.

Scott, John 2012. *Social Network Analysis. Third Edition.* London: Sage.

Scott, John and Griff, Catherine 1984. *Directors of Industry.* Cambridge: Polity Press.

Scott, John and Hughes, Michael 1976. 'Ownership and control in a satellite economy: a discusssion from Scottish data'. *Sociology* 10, 1.

Scott, John and Hughes, Michael 1980. *The Anatomy of Scottish Capital.* London: Croom Helm.

Smith, David and White, Douglas 1992. 'Structure and dynamics of the global economy. Network analysis of international trade, 1965–1980'. *Social Forces* 70: 857–893.

Snijders, Thomas A. B., Steglich, C.E.G. and van de Bunt, G.G. 2010. 'Introduction to actor-based models for network dynamics'. *Social Networks* 32: 44–60.

Spencer, Liz and Pahl, Ray 2006. *Rethinking Friendship. Hidden Solidarities Today.* Princeton, NJ: Princeton University Press.

Stanworth, Philip and Giddens, Anthony 1975. 'The modern corporate economy' in Scott, J. (ed.) *The Sociology of Elites, Volume 1.* Aldershot: Edward Elgar, 1990.

Stark, Rodney 1996. *The Rise of Christianity: A Sociologist Reconsiders History.* Princeton, NJ: Princeton University Press.

Stokman, Frans, Ziegler, Rolf and Scott, John (eds.). 1985. *Networks of Corporate Power.* Cambridge: Polity Press.

Sweezy, Paul M. 1939. 'Interest Groups in the American Economy' in Sweezy, P.M. (ed.) *The Present as History*. New York: Monthly Review Press, 1953.

Tarde, Gabriel 1890. *The Laws of Imitation*. New York: H. Holt and Co., 1903.

Tönnies, Ferdinand 1887. *Community and Association*. London: Routledge and Kegan Paul, 1955 (based on the 1912 edition).

Travers, Jeffrey and Milgram, Stanley 1969. 'An experimental study of the small world problem'. *Sociometry* 32, 4: 425–43.

US Congress 1913. *House Committee on Banking and Currency. Money trust investigation. [The Pujo Report.]* Washington: Government Printing Office.

Valente, Tom W. 1995. *Network Models of the Diffusion of Innovations*. Cresskill, NJ: Hampton Press.

Wallman, Sandra 1984. *Eight London Households*. London: Tavistiock Publications.

Warner, W. Lloyd 1963. *Yankee City*. New Haven: Yale University Press.

Warner, W. Lloyd and Low, J. O. 1947. *The Social System of A Modern Factory*. New Haven: Yale University Press.

Warner, W. Lloyd and Lunt, P. S. 1941. *The Social Life of a Modern Community*. New Haven: Yale University Press.

Warner, W. Lloyd and Lunt, P. S. 1942. *The Status System of a Modern Community*. New Haven: Yale University Press.

Warner, W. Lloyd and Unwalla, Darab B. 1967. 'The system of interlocking directorates' in Warner, W.L., Unwalla, D.B. and Trimm, J.H. (eds.) *The Emergent American Society: Volume 1. Large-Scale Organizations*. New Haven: Yale University Press, 1967.

Warner, W. LLoyd and Srole, Leo 1945. *The Social Systems of American Ethnic Groups*. New Haven: Yale University Press.

Wasserman, Stanley 1980. 'Analyzing social networks as stochastic processes'. *Journal of the American Statistical Association* 75: 280–294.

Wasserman, Stanley and Pattison, Philippa 1996. 'Logit models and logistic regressions for social networks: I. An introduction to Markov random graphs and p*'. *Psychometrika* 60: 401–26.

Watts, Duncan 1999. *Small Worlds: The Dynamics of Networks Between Order and Randomness*. Princeton: Princeton University Press.

Watts, Duncan 2003. *Six Degrees. The Science of a Connected Age*. New York: W. W. Norton.

Watts, Duncan J. and Strogatz, Steven H. 1998. 'Collective Dynamics of "Small-World" Networks'. *Nature* 393: 440–2.

Wellman, Barry 1979. 'The community question: the intimate networks of East Yorkers'. *American Journal of Sociology* 84: 1201–31.

Wellman, Barry and Hogan, Bernie 2006. 'Connected lives: the project' in Purcell, J. (ed.) *Networked Neighbourhoods*. London: Springer-Verlag, 2006.

White, Douglas and Reitz, K. P. 1983. 'Group and semi-group homomorphisms on networks of relations'. *Social Networks* 5.

White, Harrison C. 1963. *An Anatomy of Kinship*. Englewood Cliffs: Prentice-Hall.

White, Harrison C., Boorman, Scott A. and Breiger, Ronald L. 1976. 'Social structure from multiple networks: I'. *American Journal of Sociology* 81.

White, Howard D., Wellman, Barry and Nazer, Nancy 2004. 'Does citation reflect social structure? Longitudinal evidence from the "Globenet" interdisciplinary reserach group'. *Journal of the American Society for Information Science and Technology* 55, 2: 111–126.

Whitley, Richard D. 1973. 'Commonalities and connections among directors of large financial institutions' in Scott, J. (ed.) *The Sociology of Elites, Volume 1*. Aldershot: Edward Elgar, 1990.

Wiese, Leopold von 1931. 'Outlines of the "Theory of Social Relations"' in von Wiese, L. (ed.) *Sociology*. New York: Oskar Piest, 1941.

Index